Think Before You Teach

Questions to challenge *why* and *how* you want to teach

Martin Illingworth

Independent Thinking Press

First published by

Independent Thinking Press
Crown Buildings, Bancyfelin, Carmarthen,
Wales, SA33 5ND, UK
www.independentthinkingpress.com

Independent Thinking Press is an imprint of Crown House
Publishing Ltd.

British Library Cataloguing-in-Publication Data
A catalogue entry for this book is available
from the British Library.

Print ISBN 978-1-78135-228-1
Mobi ISBN 978-1-78135-229-8
ePub ISBN 978-1-78135-230-4
ePDF ISBN 978-1-78135-231-1

Printed and bound in the UK by
Bell & Bain Ltd, Thornliebank, Glasgow

For

R,M,A,L,A

Contents

Contents

Acknowledgements

On my team

In a time when we need influential and thoughtful educators, I would like to thank those influential and thoughtful people who have inspired me to develop as an educator; who have listened to me, taken a chance on me, and who have backed me (even when they hadn't a clue what I was ranting on about).

I have named here educators in the widest sense of the word. Here are head teachers, curriculum leaders, independent thinkers, teacher trainers, experts, local education authority (LEA) advisors, authors, consultant speakers and classroom teachers. But each is an educator. Some taught me to shut up and listen, some taught me to speak up, and all of them opened my eyes to what I might achieve.

If your school had all of my team on board, you'd have a brilliant school.

Alan Wayment   Damian Cooper
Rod Owen   Aldo Manino
Nick Hall   Val Fraser
Jon Oswald   Gill Murray
Robin Stewart   Hywel Roberts
Trevor Sutcliffe   Ian Gilbert
Judith Millington

Thank you.

Foreword

In his 2013 paper 'Exposing the intricacies of pre-service teacher education',[1] Australian academic Neil Hooley suggests: 'In the main ... the current generation of teachers has only known neoliberal economics and the prevailing demands of market values in education.'

This is significant. And it is one of the reasons Martin is exhorting new teachers to think before they teach in this important book.

In the 'old days', which Hooley puts at being before the 1980s, things were a little different. It was in the 1980s that the neoliberal ideas of Milton Friedman started to gain impetus in the USA and then the UK, ushered in by Ronald Reagan and Margaret Thatcher respectively. (Ideas that had been tested first in the US-backed brutality of Pinochet's dictatorship in Chile.) Prior to then, education in England had been, albeit briefly, about community, collegiality, cooperation and the great comprehensive ideal of teaching children from all backgrounds and of all abilities together. Of course, this system had many flaws, and there are as many people looking back on their schooldays in despair as there are those who hark back to a Golden Age of comprehensive education when milk was free and the daughters of factory managers rubbed up against the sons of factory workers (without ever quite making it to the same social circles as the offspring of shopkeepers).

But then children changed. They became numbers.

---

1   N. Hooley, Exposing the intricacies of pre-service teacher education: Incorporating the insights of Freire and Bourdieu. *Review of Education* 1(2) (2013): 125–158.

What the Conservative Party started, New Labour continued with gusto, championed by Michael 'What's wrong with counting beans?' Barber and his 'deliverology' principles. Then educational improvement, leadership and assessment truly became a numbers game. In the unofficial motto of management consultants McKinsey & Company, where Barber later worked: 'Everything can be measured, and what is measured can be managed.'

'Education, education, education' became the process by which teachers implemented the practices of government experts to generate data sets that would tell the world, through league tables, how well they were doing. Notice that what was *not* called into question were the practices sent down from on high. They were immutable and people like Barber, and Tony Blair, were convinced of their own righteousness. As Sir Tim Brighouse is quoted as saying of Barber: 'I've always enjoyed bouncing ideas around with him. But I could never be as convinced as he is that my ideas are right.'[2]

In other words, if schools and teachers failed to deliver, the failure was theirs. Let the naming and shaming begin.

In this model, parents became 'consumers', 'choice' became their way of telling schools exactly what they thought of them, and 'competition', the neoliberals' magic wand of choice, became the weapon that would force schools to improve. Market values reigned and education improved. Michael Barber's graphs said so.

One aspect of neoliberal doctrine is what is called 'rational selfishness' – the idea that if everyone looks after themselves then everyone will benefit. It's a bit like driving a car in Italy, where you are advised to never use the rear-view mirror. Just watch the front of your car and, as long as everyone else does the same, you will get to work without

---

2 Quoted in P. Wilby, Mad professor goes global. *Guardian*, Tuesday 14 June 2011. Available at: http://www.theguardian.com/education/2011/jun/14/michael-barber-education-guru.

incident.[3] It is using such a system that will ensure, as Gove pointed out to the parliamentary subcommittee on education,[4] that *all* schools will become above average. Next up, the committee interviews Ayn Rand and Franz Kafka on why disabled people should try harder.

It is with this model that teachers entering the classroom today have grown up, one in which they too have been numbers in the schools market, numbers that have been translated into data that have made their school 'better' than the school down the road. A system where inputs – the pre-packaged curriculum – and outputs – measurable data such as exam results – have been what education is all about.

But this is *not* what education is all about. *Children* are what education is all about.

This book is Martin's call to put the living, beating, topsy-turvy, unpredictable, infuriating, ultimately lovable child's heart back into a process that seems to have pursued the counting of beans at the expense of what really counts. It is his way of imploring all teachers, not just new ones, never to lose sight of the child in the classroom because, if we do, then we miss the opportunities, here and now, to make that classroom a magical place, with memories that will last long after the test scores have been forgotten. It is a book written

---

3 Road traffic accident death rate per 100,000 in UK – 4.8. Road traffic accident death rate per 100,000 in Italy – 8.4 (World Health Organization, 2011).

4 Uncorrected transcript of oral evidence:
(Q98) Chair: One is: if 'good' requires pupil performance to exceed the national average, and if all schools must be good, how is this mathematically possible?
Michael Gove: By getting better all the time.
(Q99) Chair: So it is possible, is it?
Michael Gove: It is possible to get better all the time.
(Q100) Chair: Were you better at literacy than numeracy, Secretary of State?
Michael Gove: I cannot remember.
Available at: http://www.publications.parliament.uk/pa/cm201012/cmselect/cmeduc/uc1786-i/uc178601.htm.

by someone who has observed the way that schools have gone, who has witnessed great people ground down by bad policy, and who has seen the life being sucked out of a process that should be all about celebrating life. Now, through his role in university-based teacher education, he is able to see a bigger picture still – not only the metaphorical cliff we are throwing children over, but also a better, more humane, more inclusive and more deeply satisfying way forward.

Systems Thinking guru John Seddon has been a vocal critic of Barber's deliverology, in all its many guises, across public services in this country and abroad for many years. He calls it out for what it is: a 'top-down method by which you undermine achievement of purpose and demoralize people'.[5] There is a place for numbers but you, the child and the moment should always come first. Or, put another way: use your data to improve your children, not the other way round. By encouraging new teachers to embrace a more reflective approach – and reminding practising teachers to reconnect with the core emotive reason they came into the job – Martin is not taking us back to some past time of shoddy practice, like rerunning the football-match scene from *Kes* over and over. Rather, he is trying to move us forward to a time where teachers are continually striving to be the best they can be in a way that never loses sight of the child in front of them, the moment they are sharing, the community in which they are working, or – importantly – their own humanity.

So, please, there's a great deal at stake: think before you teach.

Ian Gilbert

---

5 Common Core: Education without representation. Top ten scariest people in education reform #7: Sir Michael Barber. Available at: https://whatiscommoncore.wordpress.com/2013/03/23/top-ten-scariest-people-in-education-reform-7-sir-michael-barber-cea-pearson/.

Introduction

I became a teacher nearly twenty-five years ago. I trained to teach at the University of Hull, gaining a Postgraduate Certificate in Education (PGCE) in Secondary English and Physical Education (PE). At the time, I thought there was much to be learned and that I was on a path that would lead me to some 'teacherly' state; that I would one day reach a position where I was a 'teacher'. On my teaching practice placement, at the wonderful Withernsea High School in East Yorkshire, I naively thought that when we closed our doors and lessons began that the teachers were all pretty much doing the same thing. It has taken me many years to realise that this teacherly state does not exist in some finite place, and that teachers are working in myriad ways. You can't become a 'teacher' and then just plateau along through your career. The world is constantly changing and the notion of what teaching might be is dragged along on the back of that change (no one could argue that the system of education is forging ahead!).

What I am offering you here is a book of pre-teaching thinking. I am not going to tell you what to teach (I wouldn't presume to know what is going to work best for your kids and I bet there are loads of people at your school queuing up to tell you what to teach!) but I am going to ask you to think about *why* you want to teach and *how* you are going to teach. This book is also designed to support you to think about what you want to make of your career in teaching; raising your head past the confines of your classroom and your school.

While there is that queue of line managers (the folk that say they are learning to walk!) telling you what to do, there are far fewer asking you to think about *why* you teach. This is a very important question. To my mind, it is a much more

1

important question than *what* you are going to teach. Regardless of government policies or school initiatives, you remain the most important factor in the learning of your students. The students know it, and they are looking to you for a lead (they never bring Ofsted an apple or want to show them a picture of a hedgehog they have rescued!). You are the resource in the room; thinking about how best to employ this resource is vital.

The basic unit of a conversation is a turn. You have a go, I have a go. We build understanding together. Equally, the basic unit of a lesson is the narrative relationship that you build with your students over the week, over the unit of work, over the year together. That set of conversations builds incrementally to the relationships that exist in the room and in the school corridors. All 'learning' stems from this context.

Reflective practitioners keep thinking through why and how they teach. Having taught for so long, I have seen governments, educational initiatives and policies come and go many times in my career. I have had to respond to these changes, but I have also had to think about their value to me and to my students. Do I do what I am told even though I know it isn't the best thing for my students? Or do I find ways of making what I am supposed to be doing more engaging and useful for students? The second question here is surely what lesson planning is founded on: engagement and purpose. In your classroom, you must be the one who knows what is required and how best to engage the children in your care. The first part of the book is about thinking through your classroom practice.

You will find a good deal of concern in this book about the ways in which your positivity around teaching is being challenged by the current state of the English education system. I think that you need to reflect on the things that are getting in the way of you being the best teacher that you can be; and, by extension, offering the most valuable education that your students could hope for. Ultimately, though, I want to support you in maintaining that positivity that teachers need to bring to the classroom. We must offer children an education of hope; that their lives right now have purpose and delight, and that the future is looking bright.

During the book I will swap the noun that I use for the young people in your classes. Sometimes I will call them students, sometimes learners, sometimes children; this is not sloppy, but purposeful. We all need to remember sometimes that we are working with children (not little exam-takers who must reach the 'level' ascribed by the data monkey!).

Today, education generally, and quite rightly, focuses on the learning of the student. Even Ofsted is now looking to judge the impact of a lesson rather than the methodology of the teacher. But what about you and your career? What about your contribution to your subject? What about your contribution to your school? What about your contribution to your own professional development? Ask not what you can do for your school but what your school can do for you … The second part of this book asks you to raise your head from all the books that need marking, and the lesson planning for next week. How are you making sure that you are a teacher even when the bell rings and the lesson is over? And how are you prioritising yourself in all the hurly-burly of school days? You won't always be at the same school. How adaptable will you be in a new set of circumstances in your new school?

Please accept what follows as the opening of discussions to have, first with yourself and then, maybe later, with your colleagues. This book is purposefully full of questions. In truth, I want you to provide the answers to the majority of these questions. That is the point of the book. Answer the questions posed and I think that you will be further forward with understanding where you are as a teacher and where you want to go next. Before each section I have listed the questions that appear there. Pre-teaching thinking is all about arriving at school in the morning armed with a clear sense of why you are there and how you will have an impact on the hopes of your students.

Teaching is an intense job and you need to step back sometimes and think through why you are doing the things that you are doing. I hope that in reading this book you will be able to give yourself that time and space to think.

Part One: Your classroom practice

1

Being a teacher

Are the things that are important to you just as important to the children?

Where do these things fit in with their lives and with the society changing around them?

Schools are coercive institutions (children have to go!) and children understand the 'game' of schooling. When they first meet you, children know you are the teacher. They know that the school is on your side. You are the one at the front, trusted to lead the students through their learning. And, until you prove to be a threat to that learning, the students will let you be the teacher.

It is your behaviour that will generally set the tone for the room. Teaching is not a noun, it is something that you do: looking, chatting, smiling, praising and telling stories. Your positivity and energy are infectious. Children will believe in you simply because you are the teacher. Your word will be taken as truth in any dispute.

'Miss, how do you spell ... See, told you!'

The bare bones of being the teacher are this: if you look as though you know what you are doing, and you look as if you care, then you can be the teacher. Children will believe in you. This confident aura is not easy to adopt all the time, and it is based on thoughtful training, on developing experience and on personal reflection. Teaching is a set of proactive responses to the needs of your students.

The lessons themselves are ephemeral. Your words disappear into the air. It is important that you find ways to activate long-term memories by making clear the importance and relevance of your lessons. Engaging and motivating children is your business.

Most schools seem to stick to rigid lesson timings.

'Sir, can I just finish my poem?'

'No. The bell has gone. Pack away. You are off to play hockey. We will come back to your poem next week.'

This adds another whole layer to your art: being purposeful in units of an hour!

And (I hope all these sentences that start with 'and' aren't too irritating. They are supposed to be telling you that educating children is complex and that there is always something else to consider) while you have important things to tell the children, you need to be mindful of the needs of those children. Are the things that are important to you just as important to the children? Where do these things fit in with their lives and with the society changing around them? If you can be relevant, you will be doing yourself a big favour. Your students will always be searching for the value in what they are learning.

2
Becoming a teacher

What should your training year add to the passion you bring to teaching?

How good were you at driving after your first driving lesson? Already outstanding across all areas of the test?

I have interviewed people who want to become school teachers for over fifteen years now, and there is one thing they all agree upon. They want to become teachers to pass on their passion and enthusiasm for their subject. I bet you said that as well.

There is no general consensus from these interviews about whether discipline should be firm or whether it is more important that the teacher establishes a positive relationship with his class. There is little agreement about whether a school uniform is a healthy approach to indicating community or whether it leads to conformity. These entrants to the profession can't agree on what is the most important factor about a lesson – knowledge or skills. When asked to characterise great teaching or their hopes for their own practice, again the range of opinions offered is vast. But all are sure that they have something important to say about a subject close to their hearts.

This is a very healthy place to start.

To add to this, let's begin by thinking about the basics that you need to feel comfortable with as you begin to take responsibility for your own classroom practice.

So what should your training year add to the passion you bring to teaching? You will need to acquire a good number of skills and attributes very quickly if you are to make a successful beginning that will inspire you to carry on.

I think that a good teacher training programme will provide you with the following opportunities:

You will have been supported to feel confident about standing in front of classes of children. This can be more nerve-wracking than you think.

- You should have discussed the challenges that this presents for you personally. You might be the type that is shy or you might be the type that can't stop talking. It is not an easy thing to contemplate.

- Perhaps you will have had a practice run at this by teaching a lesson in front of your fellow student teachers. No one enjoys this activity much at the time, but its benefits are quickly realised.

- Perhaps you have had the opportunity to video-record this 'lesson' and reflect on what you see. You should try to video your lessons throughout your career. Keep the old ones as well, so that you can see how you are progressing.

You should have been shown how to plan a lesson (short-term planning). You must understand how you will connect lessons to make a purposeful scheme of work (medium-term planning). You must work out how your sequences of lessons will form a whole year plan (long-term planning).

- You should have worked with a tutor to construct a lesson plan. In schools, you should have experienced a mix of using your own plans and also those that exist in your department.

- You should have worked with your fellow student teachers to construct a medium-term plan, thinking about how individual lessons are part of a sequence.

Once you have grasped this, lesson planning becomes clearer and less onerous. You no longer see the planning of a lesson in isolation. It becomes less of an 'event' each time.

- Perhaps you could consider the place of individual plans across the subject curriculum for a year.

- Perhaps you could think through how your subject/lesson might be cross-curricular in nature and the potential of your lesson and scheme for creating opportunities to work collaboratively with other departments. This is a great way to meet other staff across the school, and to be quickly accepted as an important player in the school.

You should have had the opportunity to reflect on the fact that your students have different learning styles and learning needs in the classroom.

- You should have been taught about teaching styles and theories of learning. As teacher training moves away from universities, there appears to be less attention paid to this aspect of developing as a teacher. It is important: you may have to take responsibility for it yourself.

- You should have worked with fellow student teachers to think about differentiation and Special Educational Needs (SEN) and how these factors might impact on the process of planning your initial lessons.

You must work out how to sequence a lesson so that your students are actively engaged and that the tasks during the lesson mean that learning is achieved.

- Perhaps you spent time thinking about the difference between occupying children and engaging children in activities in the classroom.

- Perhaps time was set aside to think through the purposes behind the activities that we offer to children.

You need to think about how to assess the work that the children produce. You must work out how to use the data available about children to support you in making judgements about the lessons that you might need in future. You must decide how and when to mark the children's books.

- I'd like to think that you had time to think through the reasons behind marking.

- Perhaps you were able to consider the difference between formative and summative assessment.

- Practising the marking of exemplar scripts and discussing how you have awarded grades and listening to advice about feedback is hugely important. Student teachers often feel very nervous about awarding grades to written pieces.

All of these requirements so far are about the pedagogy of teaching. In the old-style PGCE, you would receive this type of support at your university. If you are working on/worked on a School Direct route into teaching, then you might have to think about where these opportunities presented themselves, and perhaps where any gaps in your experience might lie.

Then there is the need for some subject and curriculum expertise (that passion I spoke of earlier).

- Before you go anywhere near a classroom, you need to practise reading out loud.

- You should be planning your choice of reading material for your classes.

- You should look at your subject curriculum and think about how you are going to deliver the content in passionate and engaging ways.

Schools will, no doubt, provide schemes of work and will take various views on how much freedom you will be given in choosing what to teach. Timetables will be organised and the demand of the timetable will increase until student teachers have a timetable that is two-thirds that of a regular teacher – and then, in your NQT (newly qualified teacher) year, a full timetable!

* Before you begin teaching, you should be encouraged to think about the physical and intellectual demands of a day's teaching.

* Perhaps you should plan the construct of a week's timetable to make allowances for marking of books, planning of lessons, preparing resources, etc.

* Hopefully, you are able to meet regularly with other student teachers to discuss how things are going, to share the pressures and joys of the job.

Then you must reflect on your own practice and the practice that is being modelled around you. You will be asked to present lesson plans and evaluations of your lessons once they have been carried out. There should be weekly meetings with mentors and the added pressure of formal observations. While it has been announced that Ofsted will no longer grade individual lessons during inspections, I am sure that the practice of grading is now embedded in schools and that schools lack the confidence to move away from this practice with their own staff (I think it's called Stockholm syndrome!).

My list of 'perhaps' bullet points is a portion of what was achieved in a university setting. The move towards more time spent in schools and less at university has meant much less time for student teachers to think. Reflection is hugely important for beginning teachers. Being a good school teacher is hard work. Starting to become that good school teacher is an enormous undertaking.

Afterthought

Student teachers are now being graded using the same Teachers' Standards as the rest of the profession. There is the added burden of being deemed either Outstanding, Good, Satisfactory or Unsatisfactory from the very beginning. Across all eight standards! How ridiculous. How good were you at driving after your first driving lesson? Already outstanding across all areas of the test? It is a nonsense.

3
Classroom practice

Will your lesson be worth coming to?

When you shut the door to your classroom, and it is just you and the students, then you are the boss and you can, and should, organise the ethos, atmosphere and learning opportunities that you know the children in front of you require.

And as the door shuts you can rest awhile from what you are supposed to be doing. (Little aside: I think we may have got to a point where teachers actually go to lessons for a rest from the constant barrage of paperwork and data chasing.) This sense that there is a difference between what needs to be done and what you are supposed to be doing has been present since I became a teacher in the early 1990s. I suspect it was thus for years before that as well. The trick is to look at what you are supposed to be doing and make it relevant to the students in your care.

- **Will you engage the students in the topic?** ☐
- **Will there be a sense of excitement in your room?** ☐
- **Is there a buzz in the room?** ☐
- **Are your students engaged in finding out stuff?** ☐
- **Are you just dispensing what I call 'old' knowledge, that students write down and keep, or are you letting them discover 'new' knowledge?** ☐

- Do they get to take ownership of the learning at any point? ☐

- Is there the potential to let them choose what to do? ☐

- Instead of telling them stuff, are there times when they could find that stuff out for themselves? ☐

- Can you package up the dullest stuff to make it exciting? ☐

- Is the point of the lesson to be ready for something another day (test/exam ... yawn) or is the lesson for right here right now? ☐

- Are we sharing the moment? ☐

- Will students be comfortable in your room? ☐

- That silent girl in the corner (yes, she's still there. And I saw her move a while ago as well. She's alive!) always gets an A in her assignments. Top marks nearly every time. Is she comfortable in your room? Is she getting the most from your lessons? Are you preparing her for the collaborative world of work? ☐

- Wayne and Mitchell are pretending to be gecko lizards on the floor of the library as they 'prepare' a talk on their pets. They seem to be comfortable, but should they be *this* comfortable? ☐

- Will you plan how you will teach as well as *what* you teach? ☐

- When you are going to explain the process of photosynthesis, what would make the most interesting approach and last longest in the children's memory? ☐

- How do you activate long-term memory? ☐

- Do you ever plan how to read in your classroom? ☐

- What elements of the lesson(s) will you be blagging/coasting? ☐

- Where do you need to make adaptations to improve? ☐

- Never mind what your head of department or line manager tells you about improving, what do you have to say to yourself on the matter? ☐

- Are there little ways that you could begin to respond to what you know to be true? ☐

- Do the students really get to do anything in your lesson? ☐

- Is there any potential for your lesson to deviate from the plan? ☐

- Are you doing the lesson for the students in front of you – or for the assessors at the door? ☐

- Ask yourself what your subject amounts to. How does it enrich your students? ☐

- What do you want the students to take away from your lessons? ☐

- How can your lesson add to the learning of the student overall? ☐

- Do you know anything/enough about the way that children learn? ☐

- Your school requires you to help children learn. Does it require you to know anything about how the brain works? Do you require this of yourself? ☐

- Why are the students behaving for you? ☐

- What would the observer see going on in your lesson? ☐

- Ah the door has swung open and an adult has come in to watch and, I suppose, pass judgement. What do you want them to see? ☐

- Do there seem to be any routines or norms that have been established for the students' arrival? ☐

- Do students appear comfortable with these routines? ☐

- Does the teacher appear pleased to be there? ☐

- Does the teacher seem to want to share the learning? ☐

- Is it clear what is going to happen? ☐

- Is there a nice mix of different activities and perspectives on the learning? ☐

- How quickly are the students moved into being engaged? ☐

- Is there a manageable level of challenge to what is happening? ☐

- Do students have the chance to contribute to the lesson? ☐

- In what ways are the students richer as they leave? ☐

- Does the teacher exude a quiet sense of expertise without having to dominate the learning? ☐

- Is any writing that takes place, including any homework that is set, purposeful? ☐

- I guess it boils down to the question: *Would you like to be a student in your class?* ☐

- Where are the gaps in your armoury? ☐

- What do the students get a lot of? ☐

- Where do they get short-changed? ☐

- Would you, as a child in this lesson, be actively engaged? ☐

- Would you know why you had undertaken the tasks in the lesson? ☐

- **Would you know if you were progressing in the ☐ development of skills and knowledge?**

Thoughtful classroom practice goes past looking at the syllabus, past looking at the resources in the cupboard, and past the limits of what needs to be done to pass an examination.

You should always be keen to develop how you work in the classroom. Ask yourself a few questions, and answer them honestly! Here are some questions that might help you find out where you stand/how you are doing in relation to good practice. If you don't agree with the slant I take on things, that is fine – so long as you have opinions about these pre-teaching reflective questions.

Will your lesson be worth coming to?

Sometimes you will know you are doing well. You will be well prepared, confident about how you will deliver your materials, and you know that your students are going to be excited about the work that is on offer. Sometimes you will 'grow' into a lesson as the potential for engagement strikes you midway through or the students take the lesson down a more engaging route than the path you had started out on. On other occasions, you will see the lights in the students' eyes and it becomes apparent that you have them hooked. Especially that one kid who is sitting quite near the front, but not so near as to draw attention to themself and they are nodding at everything you say. Hanging on every word. The trick is to pass that engagement on from the nodding kid to the rest.

Will you engage the students in the topic?

Too often I see lessons that students are able to get through without ever really engaging or being stimulated, because they are merely being occupied. An example might be handing out a worksheet that asks the student to retrieve ten pieces of information and write them down in sentences in their exercise book. This is fairly standard pen-and-paper information retention stuff from the days before the internet. The problem here is that your students can be quite content to jot down the information you want without really thinking about it or putting it into the context you hoped for. They can continue with the interests in their lives, happily chatting away about the world outside the classroom. Walk round your room when students are doing this kind of work; you'll hear all sorts of interesting stuff (just not much about what they are supposed to be engaging with).

Will there be a sense of excitement in your room?

Is there a buzz in the room? Are your students engaged in finding out stuff? Are you just dispensing what I call 'old' knowledge, that students write down and keep, or are you letting them discover 'new' knowledge? Do they get to take ownership of the learning at any point? Is there the potential to let them choose what to do? Instead of telling them stuff, are there times when they could find that stuff out for themselves? Can you package up the dullest stuff to make it exciting? 'Today, kids, I need a volunteer to be a superhero with extraordinary powers – meet Apostrophe Man/Woman', etc. Is the point of the lesson to be ready for something another day (test/exam ... yawn) or is the lesson for right here right now? Are we sharing the moment?

Will students be comfortable in your room?

That silent girl in the corner (yes, she's still there. And I saw her move a while ago as well. She's alive!) always gets an A in her assignments. Top marks nearly every time. Is she comfortable in your room? Is she getting the most from your lessons? Are you preparing her for the collaborative world of work? Wayne and Mitchell are pretending to be gecko lizards on the floor of the library as they 'prepare' a talk on their pets. They seem to be comfortable, but should they be *this* comfortable?

Will you plan how you will teach as well as *what* you teach?

This, I think, is the key to building a successful environment for learning. When you are going to explain the process of photosynthesis, what would make the most interesting approach and last longest in the children's memory? How do you activate long-term memory?

For example, I've seen lots of lesson plans which include the reading of text: for example, following a recipe in food technology, examining an experiment in science, reading the next chapter of a novel in English, reading a first-hand account in history. Do you ever plan how to read in your classroom? The drama, the intonation, the emphasis, the questioning around ideas and concepts – all are crucial to the impact that your shared reading will have. Don't just plan what to read: also plan *how* to do that reading.

What elements of the lesson(s) will you be blagging/coasting?

Come on, you know it! Sometimes you haven't got a clue what you're doing. You're blagging. You're not really all that sure what the point of it is, and whether there is any credit/benefit to be gained from this lesson. No one but you can fix this aspect of your teaching. Rather than doing this, it's better to have a real sense of purpose and value in each lesson.

Where do you need to make adaptations to improve?

Never mind what your head of department or line manager tells you about improving, what do you have to say to yourself on the matter? Are there little ways that you could begin to respond to what you know to be true? For example, let's say that you notice that you seem to be doing all the work in the lessons, and you spend most of the lesson standing at the front 'lecturing' the students. If you were to try to make wholesale changes by hardly ever standing at the front and by never 'lecturing', the students would notice and think it strange. But you could make small adjustments as you move to a more democratic learning space. Plan to speak a little less. Look for ways that the students can be involved in gaining the necessary ideas and information in other ways than just you talking. Build in opportunities for students to listen to each other rather than you. But do it gradually.

Do the students really get to do anything in your lesson?

Research suggests that teachers ask virtually all the subject-specific questions in most lessons. Students tend to be limited to a handful of questions. This strikes me as peculiar, although I can understand how we have come to this situation. Teachers will have a sense of where they need students' understanding to be at the end of a lesson/end of a scheme of work/before a test. This will lead them to 'guide' students in the right direction. Leading questions point to the 'right' understandings. Too often in lessons, the format is set, the sentence stem begun, and the answer evident in the question. This 'safety first' approach tends to miss out the active thinking processes that students could undergo to get to the same point. The difference, in my opinion, is that the understanding is embedded in the student – not in their notebook. This is an important distinction when you come to think of education in schools being the start of lifelong learning. Embedded learning will travel with the student, while school books will end up in the bin or the attic.

Is there any potential for your lesson to deviate from the plan?

I genuinely can't remember the name of the novel that I had to abandon once when I was 'teaching' it to a Year 9 class. If I could remember, I'd tell you, so you could avoid it. I looked up and I could see that, although the students were behaving well, they were bored as bored could be. To be fair, I was bored as well – and that is not a good sign. The mood of the room will usually go with the mood of the teacher. So I said, 'We aren't enjoying this, are we?' The inevitable answer came back, so I ditched the novel on the spot. Not a great technique for saving planning time, but it demonstrates to your students that you are (a) human and (b) on their side. Respect is earned in all sorts of ways. One such way is to negotiate with students about what we are doing. Change what doesn't work; add what you know will.

Are you doing the lesson for the students in front of you – or for the assessors at the door?

Increasingly, it seems that this takes courage. The food chain of anxiety is pretty anxious by the time it gets to the classroom teacher. Ofsted judgements, head teacher expectations, head of department frustrations are all howling at your door (phew! Just as well the door is closed!). Ask yourself what your subject amounts to. How does it enrich your students? What do you want them to take away from your lessons? How can your lesson add to the learning of the student overall? I bet none of your answers are about passing an examination. I bet your answers are about fascination and insight and learning and curiosity. Let's hope so, anyway.

Do you know anything/enough about the way that children learn?

Your school requires you to help children learn. Does it require you to know anything about how the brain works? Do you require this of yourself? Keep up with research. Perhaps this can be done through joining your subject's professional association. Perhaps it can be done through attending conferences. Perhaps it can be done through going to lunchtime teacher–learner groups. Perhaps you could make use of the fact that you are an alumni at your university.

Why are the students behaving for you?

The naughtiest kids I have ever taught have generally been decent with me. I think I learned the trick one time when I had a student who appeared entirely disengaged with school. The sort of kid who is physically at school but somehow not there at all. (I know that is a fragment of a sentence but it says just what I wanted to say. So fragment it will stay!) I hope you know what I mean by that. You have to watch out for that type of kid. They are wasting their time but also having their time wasted for them. Anyway, I saw him in the local newspaper sports section, proudly displaying a fish he'd caught in a competition. When I saw him the next day I said, 'What were you doing in my newspaper last night?' He grinned proudly. I went on, 'I paid thirty pence for that paper. If I want to see you, I'll come in here and see you for nowt, thank you very much!'

And simple as that I have a mate through his school years. When I see him about all I have to do now and again is show a fleeting interest in his fishing. Instant respect because I took an interest in the thing that drives him the most. He's not a problem for me because he views me to be on his side. Same for the Goth kids when I talk about songs they have heard and like. Same when I express an interest in the work of Girl Guide leaders and St John Ambulance trainees and battle re-enactment people etc. You might think this is hardly rocket science but you'd be surprised how few teachers bother to get to know their students enough to get to the real distinctive bit about them. The bit that makes them them. The bit that drives them on.

You can apply this principle to groups of students as well. Engineer the learning to allow the students to take ownership of what is going on. If you are teaching about the Second World War, let them find out how the war impacted on their own families, let them find out how it felt to be a soldier, let them make wartime recipes and sing wartime songs.

What would the observer see going on in your lesson?

Ah, the door has swung open and an adult has come in to watch and, I suppose, pass judgement. What do you want them to see?

I observe many lessons at the moment, so I will tell you what I look for when I observe. I like to see if the students seem pleased to be there when they arrive. Do there seem to be any routines or norms that have been established for the students' arrival? Do students appear comfortable with these routines? Does the teacher appear pleased to be there? Does the teacher seem to want to share the learning? Is it clear what is going to happen? Is there a nice mix of different activities and perspectives on the learning? How quickly are the students moved into being engaged? Is there a manageable level of challenge to what is happening? Do students have the chance to contribute to the lesson? In what ways are the students richer as they leave? Does the teacher exude a quiet sense of expertise without having to dominate the learning? Is any writing that takes place, including any homework that is set, purposeful?

Afterwards, I like to know if the teacher can tell me how the lesson I have just watched fits into the sequence of lessons around it. I also like to see what the teacher feels has been achieved in the lesson and what needs attention.

And that is about it. Enough for one day, I think.

I guess it boils down to the question: *Would you like to be a student in your class?* I think this is a useful way to reflect on the range of questions I have just posed. Where are the gaps in your armoury? What do the students get a lot of? Where do they get short-changed? Would you, as a child in this lesson, be actively engaged? Would you know why you had undertaken the tasks in the lesson? Would you know if you were progressing in the development of skills and knowledge?

4

Building in what matters

Can we nurture habits of
mind in our classrooms?

Can we offer students more long-term
project work?

Can we offer them more collaborative
work so that they rely on each other to do
a good job?

Can we revisit work after it has been
completed to measure its qualities?

Instead of asking what things are, let's
ask what they could/might be. Instead of
'what is two add two?' let's ask 'what could
two add two be?'

Can we invite students to stand back and
have a look at their own thinking?

Can we mobilise prior learning to the
advantage of current learning?

How will we make use of what
has been embedded?

Can we make these skills explicit during the learning process?

Do you actively plan for these things?

Does your lesson support your students in exploring possibilities and going past the obvious?

Can we, as educators, inspire our children to marvel at the world and the wondrous things in it?

What of the unknown and the possibilities of life?

The twenty-first century is going to offer endless possibilities to those that are ready for it. Will your students be ready?

Can you create in your students an openness to new experiences?

Can you get them to admit to ignorance? Can you get them to rationalise about mistakes?

Most teachers have a desire to communicate passion for their subjects and enthusiasms across the curriculum. Hopefully, we supplement the curriculum with our enthusiasms outside its remit sometimes. I think we need to add to this an appreciation of what students need. And what do they need?

Costa and Kallick suggest that students need to be encouraged to develop what they call 'habits of mind'. They suggest that these habits will help the brain become more muscular. There is a sense here that intelligence is grow-able. This is a very important idea. Education has long considered students to have amounts of intelligence and the perspective has been that the amounts are fairly fixed. The whole idea of national curriculum levels is based around students developing along a fixed path from one level to another based on a notional capacity to learn. New scientific studies of the brain would suggest that this is not the case, and that students, and the rest of humanity for that matter, are capable of growing intelligence. School data monkeys, take note: it seems you have been misinformed about the value of your figures! Grow-able intelligence recognises the key importance of students wanting to learn and the role played by the environment of learning.

Costa and Kallick propose sixteen habits of mind that we can foster[1]. I love this idea! Can we nurture habits of mind in our classrooms? See what you think. The headings below are theirs; the commentary is mine.

Persisting

All too often I see work in children's exercise books that is unfinished. There doesn't seem to be any implication or sanction attached to this. Students can quickly tune into whether the teacher is demanding or not, and they will produce what is required, rather than what they are capable of. Also, I see too many students being praised for homework and class work that is frankly next to nothing. The same applies in lessons when praise rains down on some very ordinary and straightforward thinking. Worse, sometimes praise is awarded for comments that are plainly wrong.

---

1   See: www.habitsofmind.co.uk/behind-the-habits.html.

This does not encourage persistence, and leads to the threshold for giving up, or for being satisfied, lowering. The modern world offers many distractions and maintaining focus is difficult. Can we offer students more long-term project work? Can we offer them more collaborative work so that they rely on each other to do a good job?

Managing impulsivity

Syllabuses are jam-packed these days. Teachers are quick to move everyone on because we have to get to the next topic (there's a test coming!). Staying calm, taking your time and being deliberate are not skills that have a great deal of space in school agendas at the moment. However, thinking around what you are doing is surely more important than the activity itself. Can we revisit work after it has been completed to measure its qualities?

Listening with understanding and empathy

The four core skills of the English curriculum are reading, writing, speaking and listening. Any teacher will tell you that the one that presents the biggest problem is listening. Children are very good at knowing how they feel about things, but far less competent at seeking out and understanding the ways that others feel. Active listening is such a powerful tool in being successful. Emotional intelligence is so often undervalued in schools. So many careers require the ability to listen with empathy and sympathy. We should go looking for it everywhere in our lessons.

Thinking flexibly

One of the main problems I see in schooling at the moment is the 'right first time, every time/shortest route to the fact' model of learning. We are often so focused on making sure that students understand facts (which they need to know for an exam) that we do not let students see the wider picture. Instead of asking what things are, let's ask what they could/might be. Instead of 'what is two add two?' let's ask 'what could two add two be?'

Thinking about thinking

Planning is underused by students. Having a long think about the way we approach things is important. Reviewing strategies and being thoughtful about priorities and how they will be achieved is crucial in successful planning. Can we invite students to stand back and have a look at their own thinking?

Striving for accuracy

Our brains have the capacity to work at the level of 'the rule of the thumb'. This is an extremely useful thinking tool at times, and helps us assess all sorts of situations. Weighing up the consequences of our actions and assessing the ethical implications of our choices are important. In school work, however, we need to aim for a more definite form of accuracy at times. Doing your best to get things right is an important attribute. Proofreading written work and checking with experts or intended audiences are important ways in which writers can strive to communicate effectively.

Questioning and posing problems

More and more research is being focused on the ways that teachers ask questions. We also need to allow students to ask their own questions and to launch their own investigations. Questions need answers and demand attention from the student. They force the learner to respond (or not respond). Questions should support the learner in becoming engaged, rather than occupied.

Applying past knowledge to new situations

Can we mobilise prior learning to the advantage of current learning? How will we make use of what has been embedded? We need to develop the skill of selecting relevant knowledge to support students' work. Students can so often compartmentalise learning, and they don't always see that they can transfer skills learned in one area to another area or subject in the curriculum. Can we make these skills explicit during the learning process?

Thinking and communicating with clarity

The choices of where and how best to reach audiences have never been more numerous. This has also led to a widening of the number of voices that can be adopted; from the standard to the colloquial. Making shrewd judgements about how to speak and how to write can markedly improve the quality of the communication made.

Gathering data using all the senses

I once walked my Year 8 English class down to the science department, where we picked up some charts of meadow flowers. We then went to the local meadow and identified all the flowers we saw there. We chose to make wall charts for the science department to display, with illustrations and detailed descriptions of the flowers we saw. We collected our evidence from observing the flowers in their natural habitat. Physical intelligence is often undervalued. Learning using all your senses and having the capacity to make use of those senses can activate different ways of internalising information.

Creating, imagining and innovating

Do you actively plan for these things? If you already have the 'right' answers that your students need, then it seems unlikely that you will make provision for these processes. Students will never all simply accept what you say wholesale without any critical reflection. Learning doesn't work like that. Each student will make his own set of meanings from the stimulus you provide. Does your lesson support your students in exploring possibilities and going past the obvious?

Responding with wonder and awe

I have worked under two magnificent head teachers, Rod Owen and Alan Wayment, both genuine educators.

Having reached the dizzy heights of head teacher long ago, Alan used to teach one lesson a week to children. I used to try to tease him as he beat a path to his classroom door for his weekly appearance. But Alan was not for teasing and, in response to my heckling, would always reply, 'Awe and wonder, Martin, awe and wonder!'

Can we, as educators, inspire our children to marvel at the world and the wondrous things in it? What of the unknown and the possibilities of life? The twenty-first century is going to offer endless possibilities to those that are ready for it. Will your students be ready?

Taking responsible risks

This is an interesting one 'in the current climate' (grr! See my thoughts on this phrase later in the book). I'm not sure that teachers or their students feel confident to take risks. Having a go is not something that appeals to a student when the pressure is on them to get things right first time every time. Trying and failing, and coming back stronger, are important in the learning process. Taking responsible risks is clearly a part of life in the twenty-first century.

Finding humour

The ability to laugh at/with yourself (as well as others) is vitally important. The healing powers of laughter are well known. Humour can sugar all kinds of educational pills.

Thinking interdependently

Earlier, I mentioned the idea of being able to grow intelligence. It is increasingly understood that one of the best ways to do this is to learn with – and from – others. Encouraging students to teach others is a powerful vehicle for learning. The individual nature of the school examination system does little to support this approach. It is, however, an approach that will be required in the world of work.

Remaining open to continuous learning

Can you create in your students an openness to new experiences? Can you get them to admit to ignorance? Can you get them to rationalise about mistakes?

It is my contention that curriculum frameworks could do with being framed around these habits of mind. After all, we don't know what children need to know in the future but we do want them to have the capacity to deal with the challenges and opportunities that lie ahead. Let's help to grow the 'muscle' of the brain. Intelligence is not fixed. We don't each have an apportioned amount that limits us. The idea that intelligence is fixed has grown over time through history, language and measurement.

Self-belief is the key to development. We have to want to learn. This is a much bigger factor than, for instance, IQ scores. Students need opportunities to face challenges, to make mistakes and to evaluate the experiences we present them with. Develop healthy learning habits and students will, in the short term, pass examinations. Crucially though, they will develop as people; whether that means as citizens or as a workforce or as interpreters of their culture and identity. Our students can be prepared for that uncertain future.

There is, I think, also a growing understanding that intelligence is social. Schools, however, persist in isolating students to assess their capabilities. This is a really unnatural and unhelpful way forward. Students are as much social as they are individual and schools need to adapt their ways to cater for this. We must start valuing collaborative learning. Intelligence does not exist in a vacuum or rely upon itself to know what to do (like in an examination!). Most active learning is observational; new learners imitate the practices of the more experienced.

5

Educating children is complex

What you teach can be so important to those
that you teach. Can you find the balance?
Can you teach important things
to important people?

Perhaps we could think about the situation
like this: you know the curriculum but does
the curriculum know you?

If there is a set curriculum, then how will
that curriculum respond to individual needs
and situations?

What about the students coming
through the door, those that will be in
receipt of your lesson? Who are they and
what baggage, both positive and negative,
do they bring with them?

Are kids who sit quietly in the
corner in your lesson happy?

Where could we take this work next?

Before we consider the fact that education is complex, I'd
like to tell you how I know this is true.

Here is a story.

And by the way, you may notice some tense-switching going on but I make no apology for that. When you want to give a story gravitas, set it in the past. It becomes cloaked in the mists of time. But in the big moments of the story, slipping into the present tense gives it immediacy. You won't get away with that in your English lessons, but then the real world isn't like your English lessons. You can also start sentences with 'and' and 'but'!

It is 1991 and the hero of our story (let's call him Martin!) has just begun his career as a school teacher in East Yorkshire (Humberside, at the time). He is an earnest chap, willing to get stuck in and try to engage his students in his English lessons. His school serves an impoverished community facing the North Sea; poor but lovely people.

More importantly, little Robin Morris (who clearly has a name like a make of car) is eleven years old. He is the eldest of five brothers and sisters; his dad has just vanished and, in his own resourceful way, he is the father of the family, fiercely devoted to his mother and defender of his siblings. He and his family have a struggle every day to find food for their bellies. He is a mild little lad who wouldn't dream of causing anyone any trouble. Robin is in Martin's English group.

One day Martin decides that he is going to broaden the horizons of his students by rigging up with the *Hull Daily Mail* in a project to get students reading the paper and thinking about the news. Every week the *Hull Daily Mail* will send thirty papers to Martin and he will lead his charges through the lessons that he has thought up. Martin is very pleased with himself. Such ambition and resourcefulness is also winning him brownie points with the senior management team, who have earmarked him as 'one to watch for the future'.

Lesson one comes with a homework activity. Students have to take their paper home and have a good read through it to find an article they find interesting. They should cut out the article, stick it in their books and then write about why they have chosen the article and what they thought was interesting. Simple but effective, I hear you cry.

The following lesson everyone has completed their homework except Robin. This is strange, because Robin is a good lad and always does his homework. But Robin has his head down on the desk and won't answer when Martin asks him why he hasn't done it. Luckily, Martin has a parent helper in the lesson with him. Kath knows everyone and everyone's family in these parts, and she is able to talk to Robin much better than the ill-equipped Martin, who by now has run out of approaches to Robin, having tried shouting and being nice.

It is twenty-three years since Kath spoke these words to Martin, but he can hear them now as clearly as if they were ringing in the air around him now. Martin learned a lesson right there on the spot and it lasted all this time. The reason that Robin hadn't done his homework is that he really likes Martin and he didn't want to cut up the newspaper because Martin had given it to him and it was his. It makes Martin tearful all these years later just thinking about the level of poverty that leads a child to value an old newspaper as a gift, to think of the emotional investment that a child in need of an adult role model could have in him, and just how wrong he was about education. *What did Martin learn that day? That what you teach can be unimportant compared to who you teach.*

Here's another story. It's 2008.

Martin has taken his sixth form students on a visit to the Western Front battlefields and memorials. They are going to study *Birdsong* by Sebastian Faulks, and they also get to choose some poems to write about. So Martin and his students go on a four-day trip, staying in Diksmuide in Belgium and touring the Ypres Salient and the Somme, scene of some of the bloodiest battles in the Second World War; a life-changing experience for eighteen-year-olds.

That summer the students take their exams. Expectations are high after the success of the trip. One young student (let's call her Phoebe) has achieved grade As in all her other modules. However, when the results come in, Phoebe is graded E for her war poems/novel answers. It turns out to be an administrative error by the exam board, and she has really got an A, but Martin doesn't know that yet – and he knows that Phoebe's dad will be on the phone about this. He's a big bloke as well!

Sure enough, two days later Martin has a phone call from Phoebe's dad. Martin begins to apologise and explain that he'll look into it, that there must be something wrong. But Phoebe's dad stops him and says, 'It's not that, Mr Illingworth. I just wanted you to know what Phoebe said when she got her exam result. She said that she felt like she had let the soldiers down.'

I can't actually say those words out loud without welling up. Another smack in the face for our hero. A lesson learned quickly with no return required. Here we have the opposite of the last story. *What you teach can be so important to those that you teach.* Can you find the balance? Can you teach important things to important people?

Teachers will learn their art at their own rate. It took me an incredibly long time to work out that it wasn't me that mattered in the classroom, but the children. It took me even longer to work out that, when teachers shut their doors and the lessons began, not all teachers were doing the same thing. I never doubted the professionalism of my colleagues, and wouldn't dream of challenging the idea that they all did a good job. It took forever for me to realise that being a teacher wasn't a process of getting to some teacherly state and then having achieved it. Teaching and learning move on. And I don't mean the lesson content; I mean the relationships and the reasons for schooling move forward. Teaching children is endlessly complex because children are complex beings.

Simplifying education is only going to lead to an unsatisfying experience for the children faced with this circumstance. The reduction of aims and outcomes to a list of things to be known for exams will necessarily mean that a child's potential will not be as fully realised as it should. Under pressure, teachers will resort to teaching what is required of the system rather than what the child requires.

Perhaps we could think about the situation like this: you know the curriculum, but does the curriculum know you? If there is a set curriculum, then how will that curriculum respond to individual needs and situations? It strikes me that this is where the teacher comes into play. It is the teacher's job to make that curriculum relevant to the lives the children are leading.

There is a temptation, if you are not careful, to think only about the lesson coming up: its content, its purpose and its execution. What about the students coming through the door, those that will be in receipt of your lesson? Who are they and what baggage, both positive and negative, do they bring with them? These people do not leave their baggage at the door. They are not empty vessels waiting to be filled with geography and German. Knowing the kids and looking at what they bring to the lesson is really important.

Here's an example for you.

Pete's a nice kid. He's never caused anyone any trouble. He slips under the radar a bit. Confidential whispers inform you that 'he's not the brightest'. Expectations of Pete are pretty limited but, hey, he doesn't say much and seems happy enough. (Hmm ... Are kids who sit quietly in the corner in your lesson happy?)

Pete's last creative writing piece is written out in full below. This work is from a series of geography lessons about the environment. This is great stuff from the teacher to make use of the human addiction to telling stories, to get her students to write about what they have learned in the context of the geography curriculum.

By the way, Pete handed it in typed in size 28 font to make it look bigger. He knows how to fool teachers!

Original writing
geography coursework

'Joe's Seagull' A Short Story

This is a story about a seagull, a poor seagull that was washed up on Brighton beach. The creature's throat was full of oil after an oil tanker had crashed offshore. The tanker had left thousands of tons of oil refuse in the water. Joe was walking along the beach and noticed the bird as he was walking his daily route. He made a close inspection of the creature and picked it up, the bird was just about dead, and so he decided to walk back to the car and take it home and rear it to recovery. He named the seagull Gulliver and put it in a box with a wire mesh so the bird could see out and get air. The box had a blanket and he fed it frozen fish and water.

The man, Joe really got use to having the seagull and knew that in time he would have to make the journey back to the sea. Although during this time the bird grew in confidence, flying around the house and garden. Joe even had to place white decorating sheets on the furniture in case the gull had any little accidents. Once the bird flew up and hit its head on the ceiling. After several weeks Joe knew it was time to say fond farewell's it was a sad day but Joe knew he was doing the right thing.

So Joe got in his car and drove to Blakeney Point. As he stopped the car, he saw it was a beautiful day, the sea was calm, the sky was blue and the seagulls were squawking from the highest cliff. He reluctantly took the box from the car to the water's edge finally finding the moment to release the gull into the sky.

Joe had dreams of building an aviary in his garden so the bird could flap around and plays, but he knew in his heart he was doing the right thing. He noticed the gull join a flock of seagulls and then it flew down and stood at his feet again, he looked up as if to say 'Goodbye, chum' and then once again he took flight into the sky. At last he was a free bird. He flew out of Joe's life but the memory of Gulliver stays with him to this day.

So, again, I ask what are we (you) going to do about Pete? Pete offers you a story that is morally sound. His story offers a world issue. His hero saves a seagull from ecological disaster. Joe has a moral dilemma: whether to keep the bird caged or whether to set it free. He does 'the right thing' in releasing the gull at the end of the story. There is a touch of the allegorical in this tale.

Pete can also tell a story. He has signalling of development all the way through. He has a recognisable opening ('This is a story about ...)', reasonably productive paragraph sequencing and a satisfactory ending. Pete is alert to the need for setting, and makes use of a number of well-chosen phrases: 'He reluctantly took the box ...', 'He flew out of Joe's life ...' and 'He made a close inspection of the creature.'

Pete can spell. Pete can make use of some literary conventions. Pete, I think, is quite a visual thinker. There is a cinematic aspect to this writing. Pete makes more use than most boys do of descriptive language. He is not entirely reliant on plot to create his impact.

While moving across curriculum subjects, Pete is able to demonstrate his understanding of the issues of ecological disasters. Where could we take this work next? Pete's tale lends itself to a number of options: the story-telling of English, the empathetic concern for ecology of geography, the design element of creating a cage for a bird, the moral dilemma of citizenship. Perhaps this possible range is an indication of the richness of the text Pete has produced.

While Pete has some of the elements of story-telling in his armoury, he is struggling to find a fully coherent written voice. His use of the pronoun causes endless problems of perspective. Is it Joe or the seagull whose view we are supposed to appreciate?

Sentence-making is also problematic for Pete: 'The box had a blanket and he fed it frozen fish and water.'

Here you see the problem with the use of pronouns, but also with a sentence where the subject was in the previous sentence but not in this one. Pete splices sentences together with commas and sometimes makes sentences out of fragments.

What Pete needs is a set of teachers who know him; teachers who have thought about his needs. You can see from this earnest story that Pete needs nurturing. He has a big heart and has important things to say. Teachers need to pay attention to what Pete writes. It is the formative assessment required to show where Pete goes next. He needs teachers who know their subjects and who are also alert to the fact that students bring different 'baggage' to the room, that they work in different ways and that they have different competence sets.

You can see from his story that Pete is 'on board'. His writing shows you that he wants to do his best, that he is engaged and that he genuinely cares enough to have something to say on the topic.

What Pete does not need is to be told he is a 4b and that to become a 4a he must write in proper sentences. By all means, tell your data monkey that Pete is a 4b, but spare Pete the inflated importance and explicit conversation about such nonsense.

God bless your heart, Pete.

6
Working with the digital native

So what shall we teach these future
generations, whose jobs, we are told,
have yet to be invented?

The need for positivity, bravery,
determination, self-belief, creativity and
sheer energy. Do we explicitly teach any of
these? Do we even plan for them?

Are children getting brighter every year?

Who will the citizens of the twenty-first
century listen to? Will these young people
listen to their elders? Or will they listen
to each other?

Does the English curriculum
respond to drafting and presenting
writing on the computer?

Does the geography curriculum investigate
the potential of tracking weather systems
using the internet?

Can you (your department, your school)
change your approach for the approach
that digital natives want?

We are living in interesting times for language, and the way in which we communicate is changing at an unprecedented rate. Our language enjoyed a boom after the printing press arrived in Britain in the late fifteenth century. The mass production of texts meant that the power of the word spread like never before. Literacy among the population increased rapidly, and information became more easily accessible. The growth of the Empire had the side effect of bringing new vocabulary, new grammatical forms and new sounds to the language. In an attempt to hang on to this booming language, we felt the need for dictionaries (in 1604 Robert Cawdrey produced an alphabetical list of words that he regarded as hard and by 1755 Samuel Johnson had made his attempt at listing all the words in the language) and then grammar books, which asserted the right and wrong ways to speak and write the language. English entered what linguists describe as the modern period.

If children want information today they can go to the internet; the most important tool of communication since the printing press. It is overwhelmingly in the English language and appears endlessly capable of supplying information on any given topic. Information is not only accessible but it has become increasingly easy to seek out without any real effort. The bonus to the child is that they can take control of content and they can range as widely as they wish. They have, if you like, taken control of the mouse from teachers and examiners. Schools no longer hold the keys to information. Information has exploded and it has become democratic.

Under these newly emerging set of circumstances, the purpose of schools can no longer be to impart knowledge.

So what shall we teach these future generations, whose jobs, we are told, have yet to be invented? Change is so fast that we don't know what we are 'preparing' our students for. We continue to support a curriculum that is largely unchanged from the late nineteenth century. The answer surely lies in the processes of learning, rather than the more instantly measurable, and decidedly short-term, outcomes of examinations. Businesses are crying out for positivity, bravery, determination, self-belief, creativity and sheer energy. Do we explicitly teach any of these? Do we even plan for them?

In the 1970s, when I went to school, the situation was much the same as the late nineteenth century. I went to school to find out about the world beyond my family and friends. Schools were the keepers of information; they set my horizons. But I believe that this modern period is over. The internet has moved forward the scope and the potential of the language. We live in the most incredibly information-rich times. Most people in this country have access to the internet, and it is the computer that now sets the horizons of curious schoolchildren. The ability of children to learn outside school has changed beyond all recognition. In the 1970s I needed to bring home my textbooks or I needed to go to the library two miles across town. Now, children have a huge information reservoir that most can access in their own home. The discussion about why exam results keep going up should really involve this factor. Are children getting brighter every year? Well, given their potential learning environment, the answer is probably, to my mind, yes.

Children are plugged into social media for an average of ten hours a day. For the foreseeable future (and I admit we can't see too far ahead, given the rapid rate of advancement in technology) that number is only going to increase. The interesting thing about this is that children are making their way in this virtual world by themselves and with their friends. While adults at home tend (if they bother at all) to limit and restrict what a child does on the internet because of e-safety issues, children are at liberty to explore this vast resource. I think that the fact they are making their way through this experience by themselves is an important consideration. Who will the citizens of the twenty-first century listen to? They are fully competent digital natives.[1] Often they watch their elders struggle with this new means of communicating. Will these young people listen to their elders? Or will they listen to each other? My experience of visiting schools around the country tells me that teachers tend to use the internet in their schemes of work to gather information. This is a limited use of the resource – basically a replacement for the library. We have the potential to be so much more creative in the ways that we use this fabulous resource.

Assessment of children's abilities at school largely ignores the computer and the internet. Assessment remains a paper-and-pen exercise carried out in isolation. This means of testing bears little resemblance to the ways that people are asked to read and write in the world of work. It is interesting that examinations remain a test of memory. The tools at our disposal today to help us store information have meant that the nature of our memory is changing. Ask a young person for a piece of information and they are more likely to know where they keep that information than to have it stored in their head. Look at the way the mobile phone has changed the way we store phone numbers. Important numbers used to have to be memorised. Today I have no idea what my mobile phone number is, but I know where to look it up!

If schooling is to remain relevant in the eyes of children, then schools and exam processes must respond to the ways that we really communicate. The world for which we are preparing students requires thoughtful and skilled users of the computer. Does the English curriculum respond to drafting and presenting writing on the computer? Does the geography curriculum investigate the potential of tracking weather systems using the internet? These relevant pursuits are not central to the narrow basic skills version of education currently being rolled out in schools. And children will lose interest because what they are offered is

---

1   See: www.awens.ca/get-know-chris-lewis.

not relevant and they now have the capacity to replace dull stuff with what interests them.

Some of the best learning I have encountered in my own classroom has been when students are designing and creating things. Children don't just receive ideas passively; they make them. They take what we give them and they change it into something that has meaning to them. The old system of handing over information that is already known and copied down just won't wash with these digital natives.

The act of reading is newly complex. Technology has reshaped how we look at a page of text. Children, largely self-taught, have the capacity to respond to the various ways of writing that mobile phones, Facebook, blogs, etc. require. They are busy inventing playful adaptations to standard written grammars. Children are lazy with writing, I hear people say. Really? If they were lazy, why would they bother to change language if it was already there for them? Children don't read these days, I hear people say. Again, really? Children read all day long. Take their mobile phone from them. You'll soon see how keen they are to get back to reading! They may not write or read in the same way that the older generation do, but I promise you that children read and write much more than they have ever done before.

The world in which our students need to participate requires digital competences and confidence. Schools need to work harder to facilitate – and reflect – this. If our students are to flourish in the adult world, they need their schooling to prepare them for the ways in which we communicate. Paper and pen are on the way out. Language changes and schooling cannot stand on the sidelines ignoring this fact.

Interestingly, we know much about how digital natives like to learn. Worryingly, what they want to do doesn't always match up with the ways we want to teach. Digital natives want to get their information quickly and from lots of different sources; multimedia, if possible. Teachers, on the other hand, seem to prefer to offer information slowly and to take control of a limited number of sources. It strikes me that this is about the teacher wanting to maintain control and to direct the learning. This is a natural instinct, no doubt, but one that is pulling against the student's desire to explore. Digital natives want to multitask while their teachers want to concentrate on one thing at a time. Sitting at the back of a lecture at university is an interesting experience at the moment. Students will be listening to the lecturer speaking while making notes on their iPad or laptop, and also taking and answering texts and checking Facebook/Twitter etc. The first time I saw this I have to say that it looked as if the students weren't concentrating on the lecture at hand, but the more I see it the more I am convinced that this is how digital natives are able to operate.

Digital natives want pictures and sound. They want random hyperlinking to explore their subject. They certainly don't want to be writing everything down in an exercise book. I think a good deal of this note-making in class is actually about recording the fact that some work has been done, rather than having any actual value. Teachers often feel the need to prove that progress is being made. Ironically, in the quest for progress, time is lost in writing things down. Teachers prefer the written word to pictures and sound, and they certainly don't want random processing of sources.

Digital natives want their learning to have an instant sense of reward, while teachers are consigned to always be teaching today for a purpose in the future (the exam!).

Can we, in our teaching, address this disparity? Can you (your department, your school) change your approach for the approach that digital natives want? It has to be beneficial. Schools are part of a broader learning ecosystem than ever before. If schools and exams don't adapt, they will lose all relevance and the digital native will stop listening. Some subjects are already struggling to appear relevant to students. Information and Communications Technology (ICT) is always under threat of being out of date and simplistic in its approach. Children are making use of far more sophisticated applications and functions outside school than in. Music struggles to keep pace with the ways that young people can make use of online recording studio applications to make their own music.

While thinking about the curriculum content of your subject, you should also give some thought to the ways that students are going to be involved in accessing and processing their learning. Your kids will respond better for it.

It is true to say that the overwhelming majority of children today never use paper and pen except when they are in school or doing their homework. This is another way in which schools may seem to be abstract and unhelpful places in the eyes of the young. Schools focus so little on the real way that the world communicates. Paper and pen are going the way of the sticky note and the pub quiz answer sheet. No more. The teaching of reading and writing is important across the whole curriculum and schools need to take account of, and join in with, how reading and writing happens these days. Otherwise, school will just become a gap in the learning of the students. The sooner they can get back home and back online, the better for them. This may not be something that you like to think about – but it is true.

7

A word about your questions – and their questions

Do you plan the questions you want/need to ask?

How long do you leave it, having asked a question, before choosing the person to answer?

How long do you leave it after the answer has been given before responding?

Can you build in more ways of sharing answers to questions?

Must you always receive the answer on behalf of the class?

Can you build in a range of answers each time you discuss a subject?

Do you value discussion enough to devote time to talk and reflection on questions?

Do all your questions lead to a certain point that is predetermined?

How often do the students get to ask the questions in your lessons?

I know that you have things you need the students to know. Are you sure that they don't know them already?

A classroom filled with planned and thoughtful questions will be the most productive of environments. Good questions will help students to learn to the best of their ability (and will help them grow that ability). You should have an expectation that all questions are for all students. The answers of all the students in the room should be respected and listened to.

Can you create an environment in which the students feel comfortable asking questions? An environment in which it is okay not to know all the right answers and where the question is seen as a possible route to further thinking and knowledge, rather than a sign that the asker of the question does not understand what is being learned.

Do you plan the questions you want/need to ask? In most of the lessons I observe, the teachers ask the overwhelming majority of the questions and when they ask questions it is usually a single answer that is required. The time allowed for students to actually think of an answer is virtually nothing. If you don't have a 'right' answer straightaway then you are probably not going to get an answer in your head. This style of fast-response questioning can quickly turn off sections of the class and leads to the same few hands going up all the time.

How long do you leave it, having asked a question, before choosing the person to answer? How long do you leave it after the answer has been given before responding? I would argue that, the longer you leave it, the better. If you can establish, as a norm of your classroom, that there will be time after a key question has been asked for everyone to formulate an answer, then the quantity and quality of the responses you receive will improve. You know that if you ask a question and select a responder straightaway then the rest of the group stops thinking about their own answers and will listen to the one that is said out loud. Their own thoughts disappear, unconsidered.

Can you build in more ways of sharing answers to questions? Must you always receive the answer on behalf of the class? If you do this a lot, then whatever you say about the answer gives it credence. Your authority means that the students will see your response to the answer as the right response – and, importantly, this will be to the exclusion of other interpretations. Can you build in a range of answers each time you discuss a subject? Do you value discussion enough to devote time to talk and reflection on questions?

Do all your questions lead to a certain point that is predetermined? It is natural that teachers want questions to lead to a certain understanding. There is nothing wrong with this in particular. However, teachers can miss valuable thinking that is outside the answer that they want. I have seen this happening over and over. The teacher asks a question and a student gives a fabulous answer. However, the teacher says, 'No, that's not it' or, 'Not quite' or, 'That's not what I'm looking for'. There is a missed opportunity here because the answer given by the student is a much better answer than the one that the teacher wants.

How often do the students get to ask the questions in your lessons? I know that you have things you need the students to know. Are you sure that they don't know them already? We seldom give students the credit they deserve in terms of knowledge. If you let students formulate and have opportunities to ask questions, you can gauge where their starting point on the subject of your lesson is. You can also find out what it is about your subject that interests them, that confuses them, that is holding them back and that intrigues them. Don't let that knowledge and interest lie fallow.

There is a lot of gratuitous praise going on in classrooms at the moment. It came from a piece of thinking a while back that said we should have a certain ratio of praise to rebuke: four positives for every negative, something like that. I think this need for constant praise has not only led to students being praised for very minimal achievements, but it has also reshaped how we ask questions, moving us back fifty years to the 'question an individual child – take an answer from an individual child – praise the individual child' model. So often a teacher will ask twenty questions, gather the 'right' answers and then heap praise on the respondents. It would be healthier to ask one question and take twenty answers to that one question. In this way we dig deeper. Use a single open question with the potential to really pursue a topic: try it out and see if it has a positive impact on learning. Thinking of one question rather than twenty will certainly cut down on your planning time!

8

Teaching to the middle

**Is everything that you intend to
teach useful to every child?**

**Are you going to aim at the middle of
the ability range in your class?**

How do you know what the ability range is?

Teaching to the middle. There is a lot of this going on at
the moment. My expression describes the practice of
playing it safe, focusing on the needs of the exam, sticking
to formulaic lesson plans and pursuing pre-prepared
outcomes, come what may. It happens because of ignorance
and anxiety. Ignorance on the part of those teachers that
don't see, or haven't been shown, the range of ways of
teaching, and anxiety about making sure children are
prepared for tests. It excludes the child from learning in
two major ways. First, they are being prepared for a test,
driven down a narrow path of targeted 'right' answers that
they simply need to reproduce later. Second, students are
being robbed of the very real possibilities that the classroom
could offer for genuine relevant learning.

Teaching to the middle doesn't even make a great deal of
sense. Research (everywhere) suggests that humans learn
best when they are engaged and see the relevance of the
things they are doing. If we limit the relevance to the needs
of an exam then we immediately consign that learning to
being irrelevant the moment the exam is over. A teacher
who says to her class, 'Well, I know this isn't very interesting
but we must do it for the exam' has scored a massive own

goal. They are suggesting that the work is not important to the child and so the child will not internalise that information. Frankly, if the work can't be made relevant or interesting to the child, then don't do it!

The middle is 'safe', easy, ordered, focused (boring!). The alternative is to find ways of teaching the same material – but with scenarios that create humour and poignancy, relevance and interest. If you make the lesson interesting, then the students will be able to write and speak about the subject matter, whatever it is.

Two teachers deliver the same module of work

Teacher A chooses to stick to the middle ground. There is a lot of heads down, rote learning that is entirely about learning techniques to pass an exam. Students are required to build up exam answers paragraph by paragraph with heavy scaffolding through techniques such as sentence stems. Students compare essays and look at the mark schemes, marking each other's work and also marking photocopied scripts. They concentrate on how to write essays.

Teacher B decides to engage the students in the topic by making them investigate, letting them give feedback in ways they choose, asking questions the teacher doesn't know the answer to, learning outside the classroom on occasion, discussing issues around the topic and allowing the students freedom in how they write about the subject. Then, briefly, before the exam they show the students some past exam papers and ask them to try a couple of these, giving detailed feedback on technique through individual and group discussion of positive and negative aspects of technique.

Frankly (and I've sat through enough of these lessons to pass comment), in Teacher A's lessons the kids are not switched on to the subject. There is flatness in the air. The students know exactly what is coming up. They are all focused on another day. Stress around the exam is increasing through the module and as the day of the exam approaches. Students don't really have a grasp of what is required and the constant marking of each other's scripts leaves the students more confused. Each lesson resembles the last.

Teacher B's students look lively as they enter the room and there is a buzz in the air because of what happened last time and the potential for this time to be different and engaging. And, it turns out that they are leaving their bags there and going off out of the classroom to pursue their learning elsewhere. They are paying a visit to another teacher from a different subject to see what they think about the topic they are studying. Then it is off to three other members of staff, including one of the cleaners, to find out what they think. Then it's back to the classroom to discuss the ideas of the real people they have just canvassed. Their homework is to add to a blog that the teacher has set up. Students are invited to reflect on how they feel about what they have learned today (it is very clear who has and who hasn't done this homework, and you let everyone down if you don't contribute!).

Teacher A's class writes fairly identical essays that represent what the teacher said. Examiners can get very weary of this sort of approach. Teacher B's students have produced essays that range in how they are presented and in terms of what they say. Much of what has been written did not originate from the teacher. There is no way that Teacher A's group will do better in the exam. They might do the same in terms of the results as Teacher B's class, but this parity was achieved very differently and the long-term effects are different as well. Teacher B's group had fun, they thought deeply about the subject, and the learning has been added to their long-term memory bank.

Is everything that you intend to teach useful to every child?
Are you going to aim at the middle of the ability range in
your class? How do you know what the ability range is?

9

A personal philosophy of education

Is the history of education another
variant of this process?

Do successive governments make attempts
to quantify and manage something that is
complex and diffuse?

Furthermore, do governments try to reduce
this complexity to a simple manageable
process?

What is actually being tested here?
Standards? (Capital S or small s? School
or student?)

Are you sure that, ten years down the line,
writing won't mainly be done by voice
activation on your phone and on your
laptop, and that you will just say 'grammar'
before you say 'print' and the computer will
change your spoken text into written text
that follows the rules of written texts?

So, does entitling every child to the
same education really meet the needs
of every child?

**What do you believe is important about
your work in the classroom?**

**Why should your students listen to
what you have to say?**

**How does the action of your classroom go
past the transmitting of facts?**

**What skills and attributes does a child
take from your instruction?**

You need to think clearly about how you feel about the education system. You are part of that system, but must draw your own conclusions about the merits and demerits of policies and curriculum changes. You need to be alert to what is of value to your students and what is getting in their way. It then becomes your job to promote the positive and to protect your students from the nonsense.

There comes a point in the existence of a teenager's bedroom when there is so much mess on the floor and on all the surfaces that they *have* to tidy up. A critical mass (mess!) has developed and things need to be ordered and put in neat piles. I think that the same principle applied to the English language in the seventeenth century. The advent of printing and the consequent spread of literacy meant that a standard form of the language was required to create a common understanding, as Britain became a country of travel and industry. With all the accents being used across the country, all the new words coming from foreign climes, a unifying language was needed. The tidying-up of the language came in the form of dictionaries and grammar books. Eventually, standard (with a small s) became confused with Standards (with a capital S). A prestige mode developed and we measured each other with this new form.

Is the history of education another variant of this process? Do successive governments make attempts to quantify and manage something that is complex and diffuse? Furthermore, do governments try to reduce this complexity to a simple manageable process? Sometimes under the banner of equality and social justice we are offered a streamlined, one size fits all 'entitlement' to education.

As an example of the failings of this kind of systematic reductive teaching, let's have a look at the new Spelling, Punctuation and Grammar (SPaG) test. It was first introduced in May 2013. All students deemed within the range of Levels 3 to 5 (most kids in Year 6) took the test. In the main test of grammatical knowledge there are forty-six questions to be completed in forty-five minutes.

There is, therefore, a good deal of pressure being exerted upon Key Stage (KS) 2 teachers to teach grammatical knowledge. The testing of this newly acquired knowledge is in the form of a terminal test as the student leaves primary school. In May 2014, the results of this test formed a part of the measurement of the 'quality' of the school.

The test comes with a glossary of fifty-nine grammatical terms that form the basis of the test. The questions are, on the whole, made of stand-alone sentences from which various points of grammatical cohesion are to be spotted by the student.

An example would be:

Dad shouted, 'It's _____!'

a) broke

b) broken

c) broked

As an eleven-year-old it is fairly likely that the child might conjure up their dad speaking to 'hear' the right answer. Let's hope their father speaks in a standard manner, so that

65

the child gets the answer 'right'. What is actually being tested here? Standards? (Capital S or small s? School or student?)

The test focuses on declarative knowledge: knowing the meaning of grammatical terms. It does not, unfortunately, extend to procedural knowledge – allowing a student to apply that knowledge, in this instance, in constructive writing.

The challenge that lies ahead for primary school teachers working in Years 5 and 6 is to develop linguistic capabilities in their students that are based on the need to communicate effectively in different contexts. Isolated grammatical knowledge will not serve our children very well. The tests are high stakes for the children (imagine arriving at high school having already had it confirmed that you are not good enough) and for the teachers (imagine having to please Ofsted inspectors with data that says children are achieving).

This sense of high stakes testing can mean that the importance of the exam is exaggerated. If a child can't retain isolated, and frankly meaningless, grammatical terminology at the age of eleven, this does not mean that they are incapable of being expressive. It is more likely to mean that, in this information and stimulus-rich world, the test is too dull to contemplate.

The challenge for the KS3 teacher of language and communication (and that would be all of us working as teachers in high schools), in receipt of these newly clued up students, is to make sense of the fact that their students have a more formal understanding/experience of grammar and to adapt their schemes of work so that they don't miss out on an accelerated learning opportunity. Presently, high schools tend to ignore just about everything that has happened at primary school. Most high schools will carry out on-entry testing to support streaming and baseline assessment management. Most English departments in high schools would struggle to tell you about the SPaG test, and most high schools do not have a cross-curriculum literacy policy that takes any account of the learning that has taken place in preparation for the SPaG test.

For both primary and secondary teachers the challenge is familiar: making learning valuable in the face of backward-looking, purposeless testing. The test is desirable to the government for the simple reason that it contains right or wrong answers and is therefore 'measurable'. Whether what is being measured is of any value whatsoever is very dubious.

Here's a thought. Are you sure that, ten years down the line, writing won't mainly be done by voice activation on your phone and on your laptop, and that you will just say 'grammar' before you say 'print' and the computer will change your spoken text into a written text that follows the rules of written texts? Just a thought for all you grammarians out there.

So, does entitling every child to the same education really meet the needs of every child? Valuing a narrow view of intelligence (academic intelligence) and ignoring a good range of other ways of being 'bright' (as mentioned earlier, emotional intelligence, social intelligence – and also practical intelligence) leaves many children feeling, unnecessarily, that they are not clever. Many of these children grow up into adults who feel the shadow of their 'incompetence' at school hanging over them. Many of these adults will not think that they can achieve the things they would like to do, simply because they have formed the impression from their schooling that they are not capable. Some highly successful adults have overcome this setback. How do you think they would see the value of an education?

All teachers need to reflect on the value of their lessons.

There are endless government and policy changes. Most initiatives have been round the block several times anyway: how to teach reading, how competitive to be in sports, whether drama is a subject, etc., have been debated

endlessly. The issues are complex and taxing. In this
changing environment, teachers need to locate themselves.
What do you believe is important about your work in the
classroom? Why should your students listen to what you
have to say? How does the action of your classroom go past
the transmitting of facts? What skills and attributes does a
child take from your instruction? Whatever the common
agenda set by a government at any time, teachers need to
think for themselves about the importance of the classroom.
The narrow set of academic intelligence needs to be
augmented through the personal philosophies that teachers
bring to their classrooms. If you agree with me that the
curriculum is a narrow experience, then you need to think
about how you will widen the experience of your students.
This is not just to do with the current situation in schools.
I have been a teacher for twenty-four years and it has always
been the case that I have had to jog alongside curriculum
requirements if I am to create a classroom experience that
I truly believe in.

10

Doubt, time and imagination

Are children best placed to set targets for levels of ability that they are yet to reach?

If we get children to set targets, are we not helping them set a minimum, rather than reaching for more?

This explicit discussion with children that uses the meta-language of education has nothing to offer our children, other than pointing out to them that their teachers are scared of whether any progress is explicitly being made. (Do you think that is a bit too far from me there? Sure?)

Is there any chance we could learn about something that we don't know the answer to?

Can we ask students to think about things of which we are less certain or that we don't know the answer to?

Do you plan for doubt and imagination?

Do you think that you make time to make the students' learning more meaningful?

A little aside: if you are a teacher who makes use of sentence stems (yeah, you!), are you sure that you are starting students' questions?

Or are they finishing yours?

Everywhere, you will find cowering school teachers doing what they are told for fear of losing their jobs. Formulaic lessons with all kinds of gormless ways of 'discussing' learning with children; dreadful sheets for the children to fill in with how well they think they have done; exam mark schemes for them to mark each other's work (even the examiners can't do this accurately, so why we expect a student to I have no idea!); the setting of targets for the end of the module/end of term/end of the year/end of the key stage/end of schooling (are children best placed to set targets for levels of ability that they are yet to reach?). If we get children to set targets, are we not helping them set a minimum, rather than reaching for more? This explicit discussion with children that uses the meta-language of education has nothing to offer our children, other than pointing out to them that their teachers are scared of whether any progress is explicitly being made. (Do you think that is a bit too far from me there? Sure?)

The lessons are crammed to the rafters with activity after activity. Two minutes here, two minutes there. Pre-starter (really!), starter, objectives (write them down every time!), activity, activity, activity, activity (sticky notes, whiteboards, lists, worksheets, PowerPoint, etc.), plenary, homework (because it says so in the planner). It makes me tired just thinking about it.

Slow down, slow down: let's have time to think, and let's not be so sure about everything. Is there any chance we could learn about something that we don't know the answer to?

Doubt, time and imagination – all missing from the current model of 'pace' and evidence-based learning.

Imagination is not just required in drama ('Imagine the tie round your head is ...') and English ('The door creaked open ...' What happened next? Aaaaghhh!). It is absolutely important in science. Businesses don't want recruits who are restricted to what they already know. They are going to want creative, thoughtful thinkers able to see past what exists to what might exist.

It also seems to me that we could do better at presenting education with a greater degree of doubt, and promote the idea that we are not always sure. Too often, the learning that students are offered is verified and correct. We are asking the students to know things that are already known. Can we ask students to think about things of which we are less certain or that we don't know the answer to?

Doubt and imagination offer possibility. Possibility offers genuine forward momentum.

This leads me to the missing ingredient these days – time. Students are being asked to know (memorise) so much information for exams that there is hardly any time to stop and think about why they are learning. We need to focus on longer-term projects that require stopping points along the way so that students can think about what they have achieved so far and where to go next. We need to develop collective thinking as well as the capacity of the individual to think in isolation.

Do you plan for doubt and imagination? Do you think that you make time to make the students' learning more meaningful?

A little aside: if you are a teacher who makes use of sentence stems (yeah, you!), are you sure that you are starting the students' questions? Or are they finishing yours? The distinction is important. If they are finishing yours, then there is nothing for them to take ownership of. They are being missed out of the learning process.

11
Reading

Do you plan the readings that are going to take place in your lessons so that they have maximum impact?

How can the non-fluent reader be supported in their reading strategies, and also access the information that is important to your lesson?

What other reading matter could you use to bring the topic to life, to engage a sense of awe and wonder in the students?

Endlessly, you hear the cry that kids don't read any more. This 'problem' is held up as the main reason behind slow progress and for poor rates of literacy. The real problem here is that it just isn't true; kids read all the time. They live in the most information-rich environment and they have access to the media all day long. They read all day long. In fact, as soon as your back is turned at the front of the class, they will sneak their reading material out of their pockets and get back to it.

The prevalence of the mobile phone with online access also means that children have become adept at skim-reading, at scanning information and at making connections between texts. They are able to quickly make judgements about how to access reading material and have the skills to edit and save what they need.

What, perhaps, is dying away is a love of books, those physical objects so beloved of generations past. A similar process is happening with the CD, which is losing favour with the young, who would rather download their music. And with the increased speed of availability of text online comes an increased sense of immediacy with reading. This leads to the expectation that reading will take less time than the hours we might have spent reading in the past. Modern life requires fast and short bursts of attention.

Imagine presenting a child in your class with a textbook, one that is dog-eared and chewed round the edges. Then you ask them to read at length from a starting point to a finishing point in the book. It just isn't normal any more in their reading lives. In many ways it increases the abstract nature of schools, distancing what goes on in school from the rest of your students' lives. Endless reports talk about getting students to have the right 'attitude' to reading; asking them to value reading. For me, this misses the point. It is the mode of reading that has changed, not the attitude. Reading has changed, and we need to respond.

Schools should be places where the written word is revered. We should be developing a range of reading skills in our students. The ability to read, and to read in different ways, is crucial to the success of all subjects across the curriculum. Your curriculum content will become much clearer if you support your students' ability to read fluently. If you are not an English teacher, then you still need to actively focus some of the planning of your lessons on reading strategies. Do you plan the readings that are going to take place in your lessons so that they have maximum impact? Be mindful of the need to make use of books, but also be careful to include the internet and on-screen reading in the mix of reading opportunities you offer. Perhaps if we can tailor the reading we offer to the ways that children normally access reading then we can help them change their 'attitude'.

It is also important to take account of those who find reading difficult. If you are struggling to read with fluency, then the purpose of reading is still to learn to do it rather than to make use of it. Like when you first ride a bike, the point is to be able to do it. The following step is to go places and enjoy the ride. And so it is with reading. If your student can't read to the same standard as those around them, then it is going to become something that compounds their sense of inadequacy and something they will shy away from. This needs careful thought on your part. How can the non-fluent reader be supported in their reading strategies, and also access the information that is important to your lesson?

Students must share your love of reading. Don't tell me that you don't love reading! If you don't, then you are in a very strange and ill-fitting line of work. And if you genuinely don't, this must not be evident to your students. Reading is not a chore that has to be got through. You need to be seen to be fascinated, gripped and delighted with what you discover as you read together or as you talk about your own research into the topic. Positivity around reading needs to come from you. Plan to make your readings important. Think about your own subject. Think past the textbooks. What other reading matter could you use to bring the topic to life, to engage a sense of awe and wonder in the students?

You need to be a role model for reading. Be explicit about your reading. Make recommendations to your classes. Personalise reading for students by making recommendations to individuals as well as to the whole class. And let's have reading that is just for pleasure sometimes; no test/no questions. Make sure that reading is encouraged in your classroom. Be the one to initiate a reading wall, with photos of the teachers in your school all reading their favourite/ recommended books.

12

What will children need to know in fifteen years' time?

So what will we teach them?

In history, for example, which events from the past will be useful in understanding the present?

In geography, will we need to make place for an understanding of flood plains and house building?

In business studies, what will be the monetary issues of the day?

Will French still hold its privileged position as the language we most need to know?

Will it still be thought that we need everyone to study science as a core subject?

Should mathematics move to valuing a more real-world focus, concentrating on bank accounts, mortgages and investments?

And what do you remember from your own schooling?

The question, 'What will children need to know in fifteen years' time?', was first posed to me a number of years ago. The venue was a conference at Pride Park Stadium in Derby, and the speaker was Guy Claxton. Guy was speaking to a room full of educational leaders (and me!). I was feeling unimportant and rather uncomfortable because of it. This question was Guy's opening line and it absolutely floored me. What an impossibly difficult question for a teacher to take in. I didn't know what they needed to know. How could this be? I was a teacher. I had all kinds of stuff to tell them. I don't think I had ever questioned the value of anything that I had presented in the classroom before. We did it because the exam boards required it, or it was on the national curriculum, or because I thought it would be fun.

Guy answered his own question by saying that we don't know what they will need to know. This was excellent news; I had got the first question right and was back in the game! Then Guy piped up again, 'So what will we teach them?' Oh dear, straight back on the floor.

The answer, of course, is simple when it is laid out in front of you. In the unfathomable way forward, there is only one skill required. Children need to be shown how to learn. You can't guess what will be required of the subjects in an adult's life. Think of the make-up of the curriculum. In history, for example, which events from the past will be useful in understanding the present? In geography, will we need to make place for an understanding of flood plains and house building? In business studies, what will be the monetary issues of the day? Will French still hold its privileged position as the language we most need to know? Will it still be thought that we need everyone to study science as a core subject? Should mathematics move to valuing a more real-world focus, concentrating on bank accounts, mortgages and investments? I don't have the answer to any of these questions. Subject content, it seems to me, may very change quite regularly. I have an O level in computer studies from 1982. Now, you know, that hasn't exactly stood me in good stead! Times move on, and the curriculum will have to keep pace.

And what do you remember from your own schooling? Facts, I mean. I remember that Brasilia is the capital of Brazil. That's about it though. All that information placed in front of me, and virtually none of it retained. And I went to school in the 1970s/1980s, when schools were the keepers of information. You went to school to find out about life. And yet all those blackboards full of stuff are gone from my mind.

For me, the idea of knowing has to be extended past the learning of facts. Memory is changing in these technology-rich days. As I mentioned earlier, I no longer know anyone's phone number when I need to make a call, but I know where I have them stored and can access them quickly. A lot of the clutter, like phone numbers, can be stored and the mind cleared. Remembering lists of the dates of kings and queens is not going to bring me closer to my heritage, and I would argue that in these days, with the internet and personal information storage devices, the task of remembering the names and dates has become more onerous and more tedious.

If, as a teacher, you hope to transmit knowledge you already possess, to a passive audience of learners who will receive your information, then your audience has never been less ready for your approach.

Governments will make choices about information that they feel will be of benefit to a child's education. You must find ways to engage your students so that they are motivated; you must make that information genuinely relevant to their lives. The information itself may eventually be forgotten or become redundant, but the skills of enquiry and the habits of mind learned will enrich the abilities of the child moving forward into that unknowable future.

13

The cultural act of teaching

What you say and what you present as truth in the classroom are hugely important. In these days of pre-packaged units of learning, this can be difficult to remember. The sense that you, as teacher, are in control of the learning and that your influence is of primary importance can be forgotten. You are a trusted member of the adult world, a representative speaker and interpreter of the world around children.

Throughout my many years as a school teacher, I have always been fascinated by the often skewed perceptions children have of what is happening in the world. In truth, they are probably half-listening to the adult world. The world of the news will make its way into your classroom and often children will be looking to you for answers and, often, for reassurances. These reassurances will need to suggest that everything is all right.

I have lived through a good number of days that were earmarked as the day that the world was going to end. The classroom chatter as these days approach is noticeably anxious. Such stuff preys on the minds of the young, and it is important not to dismiss their fears as you reassure your students that the world will not end at the predicted time.

More serious events will require your comment. Children will want to know what you think about all sorts of political events and social trends. Wars, austerity, tragic events, media misdemeanours by the famous and the rise of the UK Independence Party (UKIP) will all require your perspective. Children cannot simply be redirected to the curriculum all the time. They will soon spot your avoidance tactic. They have asked their own questions. They need answers.

You have to be judicious about answering. Some things – racism, bullying, sexism and homophobia – are always wrong, and that makes them fairly safe ground for your discussions. An issue such as immigration and the rising population of Britain, on the other hand, needs to be dealt with evenly. You must not lead students down narrow paths of thinking around such important debates. Students will bring in their own perspectives, perhaps based on what they hear at home. You must counter views that are not acceptable but allow debate around those that merit further consideration. Not an easy task.

You need also to think through the assumptions that lie in your teacher talk. Your classroom discourse will be laden with your own perspectives. 'The BBC is the best source of information about the war' and, 'Of course you will get a good job if you pass all your exams' and, 'I wouldn't trust politicians as far as I could throw them.'

The whole concept of children as decision-makers is at stake here. Your assumptions will be taken up as truth if you are not careful. Be open to discussion and to the possibility of differing views – differing versions of your truth. The sense of you being right all the time comes from the fact that you are in charge in the room. After all, you are the teacher and the students will follow where you lead.

14

'Your mind is shaped by your environment'

What do the walls of your classroom say about learning with you?

What messages surround you about the value of spending time in this place with you?

How does the furniture include or exclude your students?

This phrase is taken from a music documentary I saw recently on television. Ian Gillan, singer in the rock band Deep Purple, was describing the urban industrial West Midlands background to his childhood. He was talking about how the environment shaped the rhythms and feel of the heavy rock music that he and his band produced; and not even at a fully conscious level. The environment worked on him at an instinctive, subconscious level. This got me thinking about the classroom.

The mood in a classroom is almost always set by the mood of the teacher. If you are positive then the natural impetus is for everyone else to follow suit. While it is true that you can't act all the time in front of a class, and that you have to be yourself, you can do yourself a favour by always trying to look cheerful and present a sense that what you and the students are doing today is going to be important. A busy optimism is a good front to have.

Students are looking to you to take the lead in the classroom. You are the teacher and they will let you be the teacher until you disprove that notion by getting in the way of their learning. Their confidence is yours to lose. A busy optimism coupled with an organised and expert manner will be a winning combination.

You are inviting the students into your classroom. It is your ground. What do the walls of your classroom say about learning with you? What messages surround you about the value of spending time in this place with you? How does the furniture include or exclude your students? Make preparations for the room to support learning rather than cause problems. You might make use of a seating plan, but the idea can become restrictive. It suggests that students will have their own space and be expected to stay in it. This may cause some discomfort when you do invite students to move about, either because the novelty creates frivolity or because students would rather stay in their designated spot. Try mixing up the room arrangement. Change the seating regularly to suit the nature of activities. Move the students around. Get them working with those that they wouldn't normally work with. Increasing sociability should be one of your aims for children.

A bit of fresh air and a change of scenery now and again is going to work wonders. Ex-students, in my experience, tend to reminisce fondly about the time they went to the field to re-enact the Battle of Bosworth, or about when sir marched them to the hall to show them where they'd be taking their exams and he talked about their futures and how they wouldn't always be at school and that the adult world was waiting for them. Or that time he took them to the café down the road to see what real life looked like. I'm not talking about school trips here, just everyday little acts out of the ordinary. They stay long in the memory.

A teacher who is busy, work that is important, walls crammed with subject-related goodness and a lesson that has the potential to be different from the last: this is a recipe for strong classroom practice.

15

Education as stew

I asked the teacher what he knew about Tatumkhulu Afrika. Did he, for instance, know about the mystery surrounding his death in a car crash, with rumours of the government having bumped him off because of the difficult things he wrote about?

Did they realise that he was to all appearances 'white' (an Egyptian moved to South Africa)?

Did this present any added interest in the words on the page and the motives behind the poem?

Why are we analysing the language devices of a writer on pages two and three of a novel?

Shouldn't we get into the story first?

Shouldn't we develop a relationship with the characters?

Shouldn't we enjoy the voices of George and Lennie?

If we develop the motivation to read the novel, will we not write better (whatever that means) when we are called upon to do so?

As I watch lesson after lesson in schools at the moment, increasingly I worry about the ways in which the curriculum is being subsumed by explicit functional skill gathering. The love and fascination for the topics at hand (what schools have formalised under the now worn-out and narrowed phrase 'awe and wonder') is disappearing under the drive for alleged skill-building. Nowhere is this highlighted more starkly than in the approaches, in too many places, towards literature in English classrooms.

Imagine, if you will (I don't need to, because I was there), a lesson in which literature is lurking silently in the lesson: unheralded, unloved, unregarded. How can this be? All student teachers, during their interview, express their desire to pass on their love of literature to the next generation.

The lesson plan says that the lesson will be all about the poem 'Nothing's Changed' by Tatumkhulu Afrika. What a prospect – an angry political tirade about the way you can change the law in South Africa (apartheid) but it is much more difficult to change men's hearts. Stirring and important stuff indeed! Brilliant.

But when you get there, the poem lurks silently in the lesson. There are just enough students in the class so that each student can 'perform' (mumble) a line each; one of the worst readings of anything, anywhere. Then the students are asked to take ownership of the line they have just read. Then the main activity begins with a PowerPoint with about sixteen poetic devices outlined on it. Students have to identify the poetic techniques/devices that are demonstrated in their line. Then they are encouraged to write a heavily scaffolded paragraph about the way(s) the writer has used poetic devices in their line.

I asked the teacher what he knew about Tatumkhulu Afrika. Did he, for instance, know about the mystery surrounding his death in a car crash, with rumours of the government having bumped him off because of the difficult things he wrote about? Did he realise that he was to all appearances 'white' (an Egyptian moved to South Africa)? Did this present any added interest in the words on the pages and the motives behind the poem?

While it would be easy to point the finger of blame at the 'unthinking' teacher, the pressure to deliver explicit evidence of students' ability to write about the ability of the writer comes from the approach the school has chosen. This is merely coaching for an exam. What we have here I call 'silent literature': it is there, but it says nothing while it is pulled apart in preparation for an examination. Where is the joy of reading, where the personal enquiry into great literature, where the joy of learning? Absolutely nowhere. What you have is children (yes, children) being employed for the purpose of making the school look good. A truth, I'm afraid. Shame on the adult generation for allowing this nastiness.

So, education as stew; a metaphor too far, I hear you cry. The stew is the literature; it needs to be eaten and appreciated. However, at the moment all I see are school systems that are picking out the peas and the carrots, not eating the stew at all. Children are not getting to chew their lessons, not getting to taste the curriculum!

In another lesson we are on pages four and five of *Of Mice And Men*. Once again the pressure, from a great height, is to insert 'skills' into the students (lucky they are empty vessels, eh?). The novel actually starts on page three so this is really pages two and three. We have an A3 photocopy of the open pages. A physical book might have given us a bit more belief that we were going to read a whole book but the fear of extracting hangs over us. Anyway, we are analysing language techniques and filling in the ends to sentence stems that direct us how to write (think?) about the techniques that we have had handed to us on a plate. Realistically, all we are allowed to do is write down the structures the teacher has provided for us. Why are we analysing the language devices of a writer on pages two and three of a novel? Shouldn't we get into the story first? Shouldn't we develop a relationship with the characters? Shouldn't we enjoy the voices of George and Lennie? If we develop the motivation to read the novel, will we not write better (whatever that means) when we are called upon to do so?

And look up. Look at the walls. Everywhere there are posters telling the students how to behave, how to think, how to write. The walls shout the approved words, the walls demonstrate how to start sentences. The walls scream at the students: do what you are told and you will succeed. You will jump through the hoops. You will have a piece of paper that says you can, although the truth of the matter is that you probably can't because no one let you find out whether you could or not. You are trained to do what you are told; first time, every time. Businesses are going to love you with your zillion A* grades until they realise that they are going to have to do all the thinking for you because you never had the chance to develop an enquiring mind.

I'll stop now; hopefully you get my point. The curriculum is disappearing because it is no longer the focus of the lesson. The lesson lacks any immediacy. The lesson is almost always a preparation for another day. This is a sickness that hangs over current thinking in schools. It comes from the angst created by humiliating inspection. This is the educational food chain of anxiety (sorry for yet more metaphor!) getting in the way of children, holding back their chances in the adult world for which they are supposedly being prepared.

16

It's International Chris Wood Day

It has been a long week and tomorrow is a five-period full day of teaching. You need to plan quickly for the day because you still have a set of books to mark and you want to sleep so that you are fresh for the day ahead. What you need is a shortcut; some creative thinking around lesson planning.

In this example we will look at a shortcut for an English teacher.

I declare that it is International Chris Wood Day! No one else knows this, and your students don't know any better, but your themed resources can help you through a very long day. I have used Chris Wood (the folk singer-songwriter) here, but you can replace Chris with any singer, writer, painter, historical figure etc. you like.

Rather than start planning from the point of the lesson and the learning, I am starting from the point of the resources. I will make the developing themes of the work in the scheme tally up with my resource: in this case, the music of Chris Wood. I have his CDs and I have some video clips on YouTube.

Lesson One:
'One in a Million'

Year 7 are doing a creative writing unit around the idea of good luck. Chris's song is about a love-struck young man whose affections are not being returned by the daughter of the owner of the chip shop in which he works. A fabulous and improbable tale ensues.

Lesson Two:
'The Cottager's Reply'

Year 9 are studying George Eliot's *Silas Marner*. We are looking at the relationship between the rich (the squire) and the poor (Silas). The song details a visit from rich people from London travelling to the Cotswolds to buy a cottage and its land from a local man. The local explains why the rich folk can't have his cottage or his land, and sends them packing.

Lesson Three:
'Summerfield Avenue'

Year 8 are doing a unit on autobiography. We are eventually going to write about homes. The song reminisces about Chris moving into a new house as a child.

Lesson Four:
'The Wolfless Years'

Year 13 are working with the Critical Anthology, looking at the use of metaphor in literature. The song looks at the ecosystem of Canadian woodlands and the reintroduction of bears to the forests. This is then used as a metaphor for the climate of austerity and how it seems to reawaken the sense of 'enough' in people and communities.

Lesson Five:
'The Land: When the Land is White with Snow'

Year 8 are engaged in a cross-curricular project (with art and music) to illustrate writing, with pictures and music, around wintry tales. The title of the song makes its content obvious.

In this type of planning, you get a breather from the scheme of work and you get to bring an enthusiasm of your own into the classroom. Perhaps I might also prepare a short PowerPoint presentation about Chris and his career and his songs that I can then use in each of the lessons as an introduction to the stimulus of the songs.

Let's say you are a science teacher. You love the paintings of Edward Hopper: think of ways in which his painting could support your work in the classroom. Let's say you are a maths teacher and you are fascinated by Leonardo da Vinci: think of ways that his drawings could be of use in your lessons over the course of a busy day.

Fill in the blanks for yourself: Let's say you are a _____ teacher and you love_____. Think of ways that _____ could support your work over the course of a busy day. You have the chance here to enthuse about your subject from a personal and different angle to the norm. I suspect that your personal input to the subject matter will invigorate your teaching and that this will spread to the learning.

17

'You punctured their trousers!'

My boss for a number of years was a very imposing gentleman who had developed the trick of acting older than he actually was. This gave him a certain gravitas and a good measure of respect from the students. He also had the habit of peering at people over his glasses, which perched on the end of his nose. When you asked him a question, he would leave such a long pause before answering that you began to doubt whether he had heard you or not. Often, he would reply with a clearing of the throat noise: 'brr'. That was often all you got. Impressive stuff, which meant no student ever gave him any grief and each was willing to listen to him because of his air of unquestionable serious knowledge. There was much to learn from this man. One thing I did not suspect, though, was that he had a sense of humour.

One day he and I were busily working away in the English office when there was a rather strident knock at the door (one of those knocks where you'd better be pretty important to make that kind of irreverent sound). In came a Year 9 girl, one of those who twizzles her hair and stands on one foot as you speak to her. She had been sent to see my colleague to be told off. As her class had lined up outside their classroom waiting to go in for the lesson she had run down the line poking everyone with the sharp end of her compass.

As she came in my colleague looked up disapprovingly over his glasses and said, 'Stand.' He then continued with his paperwork. Eventually he closed his notebook, looked up and said, 'Are you the girl that pokes boys?' Now there has been a lasting effect on me here. I remember it as if it were yesterday rather than the fifteen years ago that it actually was. The girl, who had come in with a fair amount of attitude on her, was totally floored immediately.

'No, sir.'

'You didn't poke the boys?'

'We was all doing it, sir.'

'All the girls were poking all the boys?'

'Yes, sir.'

I am facing the wall and pinching the soft area behind my knee so that I don't burst out laughing. My elderly esteemed colleague is teaching me a lesson in behaviour management while bringing the young girl down the few pegs she undoubtedly needs to come down.

'You punctured their trousers.'

'No, sir!' (with rising alarm)

'Did they remove their trousers?'

'No, sir.'

'Then you punctured their trousers.'

'Yes, sir.' Game over.

I never did see the child again. I looked for her but she was gone. Perhaps she left the school, but more likely she just didn't look the same any more.

To develop as a teacher you need to look up and see what is going on around you. There will always be people who are teaching you about the art of teaching, or in this case the art of telling someone off. You may or may not think this example of telling off is appropriate, but you can always have a view. Telling people off does not come naturally to people entering the teaching profession. Why should it? It is unlikely that you will have spent the preceding few years habitually telling people off. If your experience of children is limited then you are also likely to feel that it is mean to tell children off.

One activity I like to do at school with a trainee teacher is go on a walk to the furthest point of the campus at break time, when there are plenty of children about. On the way there I tell students off for the misdemeanours we see en route. On the way back I get the trainee teacher to tell students off; practising the fine art of telling kids off!

18

You are a learner too

The needs of your students are changing rapidly. Mostly, I think, your students need a guide to the modern world. While opportunity is all around them, your students need support in making informed and healthy choices. They need you to be clear about the possibilities and opportunities that they can reach for. You need to offer hope that the adult world that awaits them can be a happy and prosperous place. You need to show them that learning is relevant to their lives and that learning is a skill that will serve them well outside of school.

While your students will undoubtedly want you to be the expert in the room, perhaps it is best to share that sense of learning. In setting the context of the subjects you explore, you can be explicit about what you hope to discover as you approach the topic. Knowledge is not fixed, and it is good for your students to see you actively pursuing further understanding. On occasion it would be good for your students to see you challenge conventional wisdom, to value mistakes and to be frank about the limits of what you know. I think your students need to see you as a learner as well as a guide. It is good for all of you to be thinking about things that you don't yet understand, things that need working out, things that mean you will make mistakes, things that will need serious discussion. It is good for your students to be challenged in this way, and for them to have you there as a reassuring presence. But it's also good for them to see you working in the same way that they are.

Let me extend this idea of being a learner to your practice as a teacher. There is no end point to learning when you're a teacher. It took me a long time to work this out. I had this sense, as I trained and began my career, that I was working towards being a teacher. In my mind there was a fixed point that I would reach and then maintain. You won't reach this phantom teacherly state – because it doesn't exist. Even if it did, the demands and scope of teaching keep shifting. It can be difficult to accept this perspective. There is a natural impulse to want to be the expert and to know everything about a topic. But expertise is driven by keeping up to date with new discoveries and ways of thinking; from actively seeking out new ideas and measuring them against your own. Conventional wisdom must be challenged. We are only as bright as we are now – we can be brighter.

While schooling remains largely unchanged since its modern origins in the Industrial Revolution, this is a time when schools are going to have to adapt. They are slow in getting started. Paper and pen testing about the retention of information is a peculiarly useless thing for young people to be channelled towards. Information retention is not the most important requirement in our world of huge databases and information repositories. Better, I think, to develop collaborative project work that challenges a student's ability to think, to be strategic, to be collaborative, to be resilient and to make use of the advantages of modern technology. In such projects there is a shared set of responsibilities, and specific tasks that will require skill sets that individual students can pursue. Everyone remembering the same approved facts does nothing to achieve our aim of telling the next generation what we value as a society or to help that next generation think about how they might want to contribute in future. Yes, your students need to know some stuff, but they also need support in applying their new-found knowledge.

So I believe you are a learner too. You are a learner, first, because you don't know everything about your subject. And second, the things you do know don't always remain fixed anyway. One of the easiest ways to show students your passion for your subject is in the awe and wonder you feel when making new discoveries. It will suit you to be a learner. Let your students see that passion. Let them see you make mistakes – they'll feel better about their own if it seems okay to get stuff wrong.

Explore the potential of the scheme of work you are supposed to be delivering; investigate how you are going to make that work fun; think through the potential for creativity in the work ahead. Make sure there is room for doubts, for imagination and for some mistakes.

19

The aesthetic moment

**What choices of words, which
approach to the audience?**

**How will you encourage your students
to think through the process of writing so
that they maximise the impact of what
they are creating?**

'[B]eauty is an ultimate value – something that we pursue
for its own sake, and for the pursuit of which no further
reason need be given ...' (Roger Scruton, 1944—)

In Peter Shaffer's script for the film *Amadeus*[1], Salieri (the
court composer) describes the moment he first hears
Mozart's music. His senses are filled with the beauty and
majesty of the music, and also with a deep jealousy for
Mozart's talent.

On the page it looked nothing. The beginning simple, almost
comic. Just a pulse – bassoons and basset horns – like a rusty
squeezebox. Then suddenly – high above it – an oboe, a single
note, hanging there unwavering, till a clarinet took over and
sweetened it into a phrase of such delight! This was no
composition by a performing monkey! This was a music I'd never
heard. Filled with such longing, such unfulfillable longing [...]
It seemed to me that I was hearing a voice of God.

In the exploration of the power of music we have an
essential truth about the nature of the arts; and, by

---

1 See: www.dailyscripts.com/scripts/amadeus.html.

extension, the art of teaching and learning. The aesthetic pleasure of the moment, when all our senses are focused and alive to the artistic experience, is absolutely essential to success in the classroom. Whether it is the performance of a play, quiet contemplation of a poem, absorption in a film or delighting in a piece of music, the present is subsumed in a suspended disbelief and the art takes the body and mind to new places. This sense of awe and wonder is equally important in scientific exploration.

To enjoy the school curriculum, a student must be shown how to connect with this immediate aesthetic experience. If you overhear your student saying (as he leaves your classroom) that the book you just read together was the best book he has ever read, you will know that you have made a real impression on the student; an impression that will last and will be translated into a newly heightened appreciation of reading and seeing. What he means by the 'best' is actually that that was the best reading experience he has ever had with a book. You have created the environment and context in which to create a deeply satisfying experience.

An appreciation of well-crafted music, painting, drama, poetry and novels can develop into an understanding of how to communicate effectively. All experience is contextual. Words and sounds and colours, and their interplay, communicate to readers and audiences in myriad ways. Students (dare we call them children?) need to know how to communicate in speech and in writing. This is part of the core business of teaching. What choices of words, which approach to the audience? How will you encourage your students to think through the process of writing so that they maximise the impact of what they are creating?

20

Kids need confidence too (1)

I mentioned earlier that you are the teacher and that students are looking for a lead from you. This is as it should be. I also mentioned that confidence breeds confidence: your strident confidence in what you are doing will develop a confidence in the students that what is happening is worthwhile and productive.

However, students also need to develop their own sense of confidence. Watching you being 'clever' is not enough. They need opportunities to know they are making progress. Progress needs to be tangible: your student needs to be able to see/sense that they are improving. Developing teaching sequences that have positive outcomes is important for student self-esteem.

In terms of the classroom routines, there is a standard practice that I observe, in lessons up and down the country, in which students are encouraged to do/experience things and are then expected to become good at those things. Do things and then become capable. Does this ring true with you? Or is it backwards on? Should we become knowledgeable about things first and then try those things out, or develop an expertise and then try it out?

Experience – Knowledge – Reflect

OR

Knowledge – Experience – Reflect

Perhaps we could employ both routes. If one doesn't work, then change to the other. Mix and match.

Kids need confidence too (2)

All the current fretting about what national curriculum level a student is on seems to me to miss the point that children have competences in some things and not in others. To say that a student is a 5a is wholly unsatisfactory (as are almost all data sets used by schools). A student will have a huge range of competences based on their experiences, the mood they are in, their physical well-being, their satisfaction with life generally, and any number of other factors.

Here is a brief exercise to try with your students that might make you think about their capabilities. Say to the students that, while you are the teacher, you are sure there are things that they (the students) can teach you. Ask each student in turn to tell you about something they could teach you. You will be amazed at the range of knowledge they display, and the variety of lessons you are offered.

21
The magic formula

Oh dear! There isn't one. Sorry to disappoint you. As a beginning teacher you will start by worrying about yourself. In those first few lessons you will prepare enough lesson content to fill a month of work. You'll learn. You will focus on yourself and how well you have done in the lesson. This is as it should be. Lesson plans will take longer to think of and to write up than the lesson lasts. Again, all right and proper. You will be thinking about the lessons on an individual basis, one by one, rather than with the longer-term goals in mind. You will focus on subject content and what needs to be learned by your students. This is all okay.

But there will come a point when you start to think about the students and how they have done, as you come away from your lessons. You will notice that Charlie seems to be behaving a bit better now that he has moved to sit by himself, and that Mary is finally really enthused about her project. The emphasis of your thinking will move from how well *you* have done in a lesson to how well the *students* have done. I think this is a fairly standard, healthy scheme of things.

Heads of department, mentors and colleagues will all offer advice. Listen to those folk; they are on your side. Hopefully, you will have joined your professional association and will be keeping up with curriculum developments. You will be attentive during INSETs, you will be applying to go on courses, and eager to contribute to TeachMeet events in your area. Your enthusiasm and commitment to the school will not go unnoticed. Your expertise and experience will develop and you will become a thoughtful and valued member of staff. (People will be earmarking you for promotion!)

Once you feel on top of the job in the classroom, you can start to extend your contribution to the wider school.

Part Two: Your school and the wider teaching community

22

No-Brainer Academy

'Brainium non necessitum'

Are you right first time, every time? Then we are looking for you! Teachers needed at No-Brainer Academy!

Are you able to dispense our pre-planned lessons that take the love out of learning? Here at No-Brainer we understand that students can do fun stuff at home – there's no need for fun at school. Can you read facts off a colourful PowerPoint and get kids to write them down and learn them? Can you put a stop to anything productive that might be going on every twenty minutes to make sure that progress is being made?

We know all the Ofsted words, like 'rigour' and 'accountability' and 'Outstanding' and 'aspire', so you can be assured that we too will do what we are told in an unthinking way.

We have brand new shiny buildings (like a shopping centre – great!), a brilliant badge and a vacuous motto that all add up to an appearance of quality. All the kids wear the same uniform with piping round the edges of the blazer so that they look like a big brass band. We also have a trophy head teacher who you only see in photos, never in real life.

Do you like data? We love data. We've got loads of it. Data that will tell you all you need to know about your students, meaning that you won't need to get to know them. No fuss, no mess. However well your results go, this data will always find ways to suggest your incompetence.

If you do have a futile interest in teaching and learning (so old school!) then there is a lunchtime club for you where you can meet with the other lefties we haven't driven out yet. Don't worry, though, the senior management team pay no attention to these discussions. There are a few superfluous lessons still on the timetable, but we take every opportunity to withdraw everyone from these lessons for extra literacy and numeracy intervention, mainly with unqualified staff. We have plenty of middle leaders who have been made to follow you around with a clipboard noting down your inadequacies.

We won't overburden you with a good salary, so there will be plenty of time in your ridiculously long holidays to do schoolwork instead of having a holiday.

If this sounds like you, then come and join us. No-Brainer Academy: creating a generation of unthinking teachers that we can constantly humiliate for their lack of skill and professionalism.

No-Brainer: a proud member of the Numb Nuts academy chain.

23

An education that touches the sides

So what is your school's approach to the education of its children?

Do you feel you have a say in the education offer that the children receive?

Is there an active forum for teachers to share their creative ideas?

Does the school invest time and money in thinking about the best ways to improve teaching practices?

Does your school look for ways to increase your abilities as a practitioner?

Does your school see training as a way of helping you move on in your career?

I used to visit my grandma in Middlesbrough every other weekend when I was about sixteen. She was a proper grandma, one that feeds you every chance she gets. I ate everything I was given, like a sixteen-year-old – fast. She would always shake her head and say that the food 'went down so fast it didn't touch the sides'.

There are too many schools whose education offering never touches the sides. In recent years, the emphasis on competition between schools has meant a narrowing of curriculum to focus on passing exams. Schools are packaging up schemes of work and requiring their teachers to follow them. The schemes themselves are about passing exams. This may seem bleak, but I regularly see it as I visit schools around the country. All this pre-planned, narrow, leading-by-the-nose education offering means there can, at times, be nothing for teachers and their students to genuinely do/think about.

As mentioned in Part One, schools are coercive regimes; if you are a kid you have to go to school. You have no choice. A series of choices is already made for students: they have to learn this, they have to know that. And in the abstract world of school, split into five hour-long portions with entirely unrelated focuses, students are quick to play the system. If a topic or task needs to be learned for an exam then they will 'try' to take it seriously. What this tends to amount to is they memorise information for the test, reproduce it in the test, then erase it from their memory after the test is over. Perhaps, in telling your students that something is important because it is for the test, you are actually limiting its importance and any long-term value it might have had.

I think that we – you and I – need to move from a language of 'have to' to a language of 'want to'. Students are very good at telling you, both explicitly and implicitly, what they want to do. This doesn't always tally with what the government, school and your department want them to do. Our task is to move the prescribed curriculum into the realm of 'want to' and away from the excuse of 'have to'. Too often I hear teachers say, 'Look, I know you don't like doing this. I don't like doing this. We just have to get on and do it. It's important.' If no one wants to do it and no one likes doing it then it really isn't of any importance.

People say the world is getting smaller because of the internet. Let's look at it from the perspective of the child with a mobile phone in her pocket and a laptop in her bedroom and heaven only knows how many TV channels at her disposal. I would say that the world is getting bigger. Much bigger. A world of opportunity awaits our young people. Choices are everywhere.

When students tell you what they want to do, what they are telling you about is threefold; they are telling you what they think is significant, they are telling you they value that thing, and they are telling you they are interested in that thing. *Significance, value* and *interest.* Here is a recipe for your lessons. If students feel what they are doing has these attributes then they will be motivated. Motivation is the difference between being occupied and being engaged. Considering the students' perceptions can be tough. After all, you are the one who comes to the lesson with the plan, you are the one who knows what it is 'important' to do/know.

Motivated children always outperform unmotivated children at all levels. Think about the difference between doing work explicitly because it is for an exam, and doing a project because we are developing writing skills because we are learning to blog. In developing as writers, students gain significant skills that they can apply, and develop, throughout their lives. I can't see the logic of the 'no pain, no gain' approach to exam preparation for the singular purpose of passing an exam. Nothing is served by preparing exam answers in Year 9 for a test in Year 11, or teaching isolated points of grammar to Year 6 for the grammar test. Businesses are not crying out for people who have the life skill of passing tests, or a declarative knowledge of the finer points of grammar. Neither will this improve a child's artistic drives.

So what is your school's approach to the education of its children? Hopefully, the individual needs and aspirations of the children are at the centre of the curriculum on offer. Do you feel that you have a say in the education offer that the children receive? Presumably, as the frontline teachers who work with the students every day, you are consulted about productive approaches. Is there an active forum for teachers to share their creative ideas? You are encouraged to share your successes and to work collaboratively both across the school and the local community of schools. Does the school invest time and money in thinking about the best ways to improve teaching practices? INSET days are all about creativity and developing an understanding of topics such as the changing nature of literacy or how the brain works. Does your school look for ways to increase your abilities as a practitioner? Money is set aside for you to go on courses and to represent the school at exam board training sessions. Does your school see training as a way of helping you move on in your career? Line management meetings focus on you and ways to support you in becoming the best teacher possible so that you have many competences to offer when you want to move on in your career.

Part Two of this book asks you to think about the type of school you are in and the sort of teaching practices you think are healthy. Let's begin by thinking about the various routes into teaching and how your introduction to the career of teaching might have coloured your view of how it might be. You need to have a clear perspective of what is going on in the world of education – and how you feel about it.

I am asking you to think about how you can contribute to an education that 'touches the sides'.

24

Routes into teaching

**Why don't we get rid of all
training demands?**

**Why can academies employ who they want,
but other state schools can't?**

**Why can the independent sector employ
people as teachers who have no training,
but state schools can't?**

**Why are free schools (unless the DfE takes
exception to the ways free schools use
their freedoms!) able to employ unqualified
teachers, while state schools cannot?**

Your training, the training of new teachers, and the
ongoing training of all teachers are intensely important
activities. However, this is not reflected in the current
thinking and government policies. Time spent at the
beginning of your career given over to reflection is being
severely reduced. The emphasis is on getting into the
classroom and teaching straightaway.

*What you have been told teaching is will determine how you
perceive your role.* There is a general agreement that new
teachers need some time in front of classes, and that this
experience needs to be shaped by thoughtful reflection on
why they want to teach; what the purpose of their teaching
might be. New teachers, like all teachers, need to think
about best practice and then develop their ideas in the

classroom. Your learning should be assisted by experienced teachers and teacher educators who have the expertise, time and resources to support developing understandings of pedagogy. I also think that you need time to share experiences with other teachers as they make their journey beyond qualified status. An understanding that schools face different challenges and opportunities is a vital part of forming an accurate impression of what the potential of a career in teaching might be. And you need the opportunity to get things wrong and to learn from making mistakes.

Government pronouncements suggest that there is a level of mistrust in university-based training. There is a perception that Higher Education Institutes (HEI) are populated by teacher educators who have been out of the classroom too long and that being trained by these people leaves the trainee ill-equipped to face the challenges of the modern classroom. Government initiatives suggest that student teachers should be learning 'on the job' and the time that is devoted to reflective practice in universities is either not necessary or should be set in schools. In my experience, none of this is true.

Schools are in direct competition with each other to offer training to trainee teachers, and each has a different 'package'. Training schools can offer qualified teacher status training but without the master's-level accreditation that would have been part of the professional expectation in years gone by. Universities can work in partnership with school alliances offering qualified teacher status either with master's accreditation (Level 7 in university speak) or, for those whose academic work doesn't reach the required level, there is the award of qualified teacher status (at Level 6; undergraduate level) without master's accreditation. It is also possible for a school to sponsor a trainee teacher through teacher training, making a private arrangement with a university to accept a student on its course. This route circumnavigates the UCAS (University and Colleges Admissions Service) selection process altogether, and is not held to account by any strict entry requirements. It is very much up to the university to decide its entry requirement here. The more cynical among you might think that, in these difficult times for university-led training programmes, money might be the overriding factor.

There are so many routes into teaching at the moment that it is difficult to have a clear grasp of the right route for any one person. It also means that the staffroom – if your school has a staffroom – will have teachers in it who have all sorts of different experiences of training. You may well find that this creates many different perceptions of the role of school teacher. Some of your colleagues will understand the need to reflect on pedagogy and will look at their own school's situation in a wider context. Some will see only their role in dispensing lessons in their own school, having been branded from the start. Having a more rounded perspective is going to make you more saleable when the time comes for you to move on in your career.

Each of the routes into teaching can have challenges. If you are a student teacher who took the more traditional training route (which front-loaded lots of university time), you may have yearned to get into schools and make a start at teaching. However, I have met so many student teachers like that who would have been best suited to precisely that model of teacher training that allows for three weeks in university before heading off to schools; student teachers who need time and space to think through the practicalities of teaching before they are presented with a class. Unfortunately, a good number of these student teachers have been on the salaried School Direct route[1] (pretty much straight into schools and onto a paid timetable), and many have come to see me because they feel they can't carry on because the work has overwhelmed them and they don't know how to move forward. Students in this predicament generally want help with planning their lessons for next week before they have had a chance to

---

1   See: www.education.gov.uk/get-into-teaching/teacher-training-options/school-based-training.

think about why, in the long term, they are teaching or even, in the medium term, why they are teaching the children in front of them this work.

It is also difficult for those looking at becoming teachers to see the long-term benefits and demerits of different routes to qualified teacher status. A qualification at Level 6 does not carry the distinction of a PGCE, which has been the quality mark for so long and is so important if you want to teach abroad. I am sure that head teachers still identify the PGCE as the foremost route into teaching. It is recognised and at the higher level of academic challenge. In these times of uncertainty (and no genuine system), I am sure it retains its value and prestige with those who are hiring.

One interesting new route is that of Teach First[2]. This route is aimed at those would-be trainee teachers who have achieved high grades at university and who want to change the life chances of students from economically and socially difficult backgrounds. Teach First is a charity devoted to getting rid of educational inequality. There is a definite evangelical approach here. The government is very keen on Teach First at the moment. It fits the 'every child matters' agenda and the idea of closing the gap between those who are advantaged and those who are not.

It involves a two-year commitment to teaching, with qualified teacher status awarded during the course. Again, the course is front-loaded with theoretical perspectives. Time is spent with both Teach First tutors and university tutors thinking through the task at hand, with a particular focus upon social inclusion. There is a Summer Institute during which the training continues. There is training both for subject specifics and the wider issues surrounding educating children. After a short summer holiday, student teachers (or 'participants', as they are called) are given a two-year placement in a school that faces challenging circumstances. This can be a very demanding route into

---

2 See: www.teachfirst.org.uk.

teaching. The level of support budgeted for here is higher than in some other routes.

The Teach First website indicates that 54% of those who complete the two-year commitment actually remain in teaching. While this may seem quite a damning figure, I think it is more representative of the aspirations and expectations of the young generally. Someone committing to two years with Teach First may well not be committing to a lifetime in teaching. The website indicates:

At the moment, 54% of ambassadors are in teaching positions throughout the UK; this means that at the same time, nearly half of the network is able to influence change in business, the third sector and government through alternative careers.

United by a unique insight into the challenges schools face, experience of what works, and the expertise and commitment to continue addressing the Teach First vision, this is a powerful network for social change.

I think the government is keen on this route because it suits their aim of getting well-qualified graduates into the profession. However, I tend to accept that schooling has to be seen in broader terms. Certainly, schools need to see that they are part of a wider ecosystem of learning. In this light, there is merit in the Teach First route.

Now let's turn our attention to looser forms of 'training' (no, really, there *are* looser forms coming up!)

Academies, free schools and the independent sector

Ah! It turns out that by 'looser', what I actually mean is 'non-existent'. In these locations you don't have to have any qualifications at all. You can be hired to do the work of a school teacher without any form of training or qualification. This does not mean that this has to be the case, and most of the people working in teaching posts in these locations will have qualifications.

You might think that teaching is something anyone could turn their hand to, and there is no need for a qualification to demonstrate you have had some training and during that training you have shown a clear competence to teach. Let me ask you this, then: why don't we get rid of all training demands? Why can academies employ who they want, but other state schools can't? Why can the independent sector employ people as teachers who have no training, but state schools can't? Why are free schools (unless the DfE takes exception to the ways free schools use their freedoms!) able to employ unqualified teachers, while state schools cannot?

Do you have an equitable answer to any of these questions? I have yet to hear any sensible answers.

In March 2013, a DfE spokesperson was quoted as saying, 'We have extended this flexibility [hiring unqualified people to act as teachers] to all academies, so more schools can hire great linguists, computer scientists, engineers and other specialists who have not worked in state schools before.'

Unfortunately, the truth of the matter is this is not how schools have adopted the 'flexibility'. It has been an open invitation to fill vacant teacher posts (created by the shortfall in teacher training places accepted) with people with no qualifications. Often these are young, inexperienced people who are trying to get a teacher training place but who need to make money in the meantime. While I am sure that the DfE wouldn't say this is a cost-cutting exercise, I'm afraid this is the reality. This is what is happening. Teachers and parents should be very concerned.

I have just trawled through the web pages of recruitment agents offering positions as unqualified teachers. You could apply for a job as an unqualified teacher of history in the Yorkshire area. The pay is £60 a day. I'm not sure this is going to attract the 'specialists' that the DfE spokesperson was championing.

One of the problems with the current situation is the fact that all these routes are in direct competition. This also means it is difficult for the person hopeful of becoming a teacher to make a balanced choice, given the biased self-promotion of each of the routes.

For over half a century before the coalition government came to power, the responsibility for making sure that there were enough teachers to teach all the children in the country fell to the government and its agencies. Recruitment was stable and the routes to a training place were fairly evident to all. However, the coalition abolished the Training and Development Agency for Schools, and the responsibility of government disappeared. There is a crisis looming because of this. Teachers are going to be in short supply. Couple this with the fact that there is not enough funding going towards primary school teacher recruitment, and the government failure to allocate places with any sense of regional planning, and there is going to be a huge shortfall.

The most immediate problem is that there is no system, no authority, taking control of this situation. Schools are being asked to take over recruitment of trainees, being asked to take over the bulk of the training for new trainees, and the expertise in universities is beginning to lie fallow.

This lack of system, lack of integrity, lack of common sense, lack of standards, will bite back through a distinct narrowing of the capacity of schools to deliver good-quality education to our children. What we have here is a fragmentation of the system, no monitoring of standards, a loss of expertise in universities, the de-professionalisation of teaching and an almighty potential for a shortage of teachers.

It all lacks grace. Dis-grace. Disgrace.

Please indulge me for a moment: what follows is my take on whether or not we need to have a fully professional approach to the training of teachers.

It seems to me that lots of things humans learn to do are by trial and error. Learning to walk, for example, is one where we keep giving it a go because we want to join in with everyone around us, who is moving about. We make mistakes and keep falling over and hurting ourselves, but we really want to do it and that spurs us on. Parents and other adults will give us encouragement and little goals to achieve and will naturally ask more of us as we get more proficient. Perhaps, though, this is an unfair example, as the need to walk is inbuilt; part of what it is to be human.

Instead, let's look at operating a new mobile phone. Like walking, we have the desire to be able to do it. We want to be able to operate the phone as soon as possible. No one ever really reads the impenetrable booklet that comes with a phone (did you? really?) before experimenting with the buttons to make sense of it themself. Only then would you go back to the manual if there was a particular function you couldn't work. But this is low risk. I think that working out how the phone works using trial and error is fair enough.

Perhaps there is some middle ground where the activity is low risk but some advice would be a good idea. Learning a musical instrument will become faster if someone points the learner in the right direction. However, the activity remains low risk.

But some things are high risk. For instance, driving a car is not something we are prepared to allow people to try using the trial-and-error method. It is high risk, so people must be proficient before we let them do it by themselves. Putting out a fire is also high risk. Performing surgery is also high risk. Giving legal advice is high risk.

So the answer to whether you need to train teachers or not boils down to whether you think children's learning and getting it right straight away is a high- or low-risk activity. Ask parents what the answer is to this question. In fact, ask a politician. You will be hard pushed to find a politician who doesn't think that a child's education is important (high risk)!

The current 'system' (non-system) is so poor it isn't funny at all. The instruction of people new to teaching is high risk. There should be one point of entry through which all trainee teachers must pass. All must be qualified and ready to work with the children in their care in their NQT year.

Think through the sort of training that you have had (or, if you are contemplating becoming a teacher, are about to have). It is important that you can see the widest possible perspective. You need to know what is happening nationally – and not just so that you teach the kids the right stuff for the exams!

25

Growing a school

**What about developing the capacities
of the teachers?**

**What about celebrating the capacities
of the teachers?**

How does your school grow?

**Do you see your school in any, or
maybe all, of these models?**

**Where do you see your responsibility
in all of this?**

**You're just the NQT, right? Do what
you're told, right?**

It always makes me laugh when trophy head teachers (the sort that you see in all the photographs but never in real life) say that they aim to raise standards while showing you their brand new shiny badge/brochure/sign. The alternative, of course, is to aim to lower standards! In this light, the championing of the 'raising' is a non-ambition; it's a given for all schools.

I am afraid that 'raising standards' tends to mean 'looking good'. While most school prospectuses will highlight this raising of standards, there is very little discussion of how this will be done in the classroom. Yes, there will be a nice new uniform and a strict discipline code. But what about developing the capacities of the teachers? What about celebrating the capacities of the teachers? Hmm, not much there!

So how does your school grow?

Below, I offer you four prevalent models. Do you see your school in any, or maybe all, of these models? After these, I offer a fifth model for your consideration. Have a think about them.

Model One

Head teachers can approach the forward momentum of their schools *through making short-term gains in exam results.* This will undoubtedly have a positive impact. Children and parents will gain confidence in the school and its reputation will grow. This will help attract better teachers to the school and perhaps the growth of the school will then gather further momentum. There is the possible drawback that lessons will focus too much on exam preparation. A genuine education suitable for children entering the adult world of the twenty-first century cannot be gained through slavish adherence to the needs of exam board syllabuses. This focus will inevitably lead to a narrow educational experience.

Model Two

Head teachers can *react to the areas of improvement that are outlined in their Ofsted reports.* This sounds really thin as an ethos, but I can assure you that there are plenty of school leadership teams out there who have no more depth to their planning than that. The idea is that if you concentrate on the things identified by Ofsted as being in need of attention (this is the all-seeing Ofsted that popped in for two days, probably with a reasonably savvy inspector and a team of folk who look like they are out on a pensioners' mystery coach trip! Only joking ...), then the rest will be fine.

Model Three

Head teachers can approach establishing an improvement *by dealing with the discipline 'problem' in* the school. There are too many children messing about and making it difficult for teachers to teach and for those students who do want to work to work. Immediately exclude the three naughtiest kids in the school, sending out a message to all the others. A new behaviour policy: strict on uniform, strict on attendance, strict on language, strict on walking to the left in the corridors. Subdue the children, make them conform and the school will run more effectively. The new discipline code will not take long to bed in if we all stick to it.

Model Four

Head teachers can *join an academy chain.* The long-term plan, of course, is to ditch the chain and strike out on your own, but a leg-up while you get going won't go amiss. Joining an academy chain means new badges and new signs that herald this new status. While you're changing things, you can have a new house system replacing year groups, and you could change the uniform as well. Why not?

Dear readers, you may well be able to see what I am doing here. *The four models listed above are, of course, in real life one model!* Imagine the school driving 'forward' by focusing on exam results, reacting to Ofsted report recommendations, sorting out the discipline problem and joining an academy chain.

This is the way it is going at the moment. High pressure, high stakes, competition-driven 'progress'! Do you notice anything that is missing in these ways forward? Ah yes, teachers and learners. Teachers and learners (formerly the focal point of schools) have become an irritation to the power-builders of education. Teachers need to make sure that the students pass exams; that is the limit of the expectation that management has of its teachers. (Is this too bleak a picture to paint? Check around you, please.)

Now, I offer you Model Five.

In Model Five, a school does *not*:

- Focus on the short-term gains of making students constantly prepare for exams and tests. Instead, curriculum ownership is given to the subject leads, who design a whole-school curriculum together, each subject adding to an overall sense of a coordinated approach. The subject leads define the purpose of the curriculum. Exams and tests are relegated to thermometer readings of how things are progressing. Data generated from tests and assessments is formative. The data monkey is there to serve the teachers, not the other way round. There is a focus on developing life and study skills so that students who leave the school have the presence of mind to join in with the opportunities the adult world has to offer.

- Spend all its time waiting for the next Ofsted inspection. Instead, the school considers what is required for the students in its care. There is a senior management role dedicated to project initiatives to feed into the school development plan. This plan is about teaching and learning. Ofsted recommendations are seen as that: recommendations. If some are appropriate then they will be acted upon. If not, then they won't. If Ofsted recommendations don't fit in with the development plan, then they won't be followed up.

- Focus the idea of discipline exclusively on the students. Instead, the school spends time on making school worth behaving for; making the lessons worth behaving for; making the extracurricular opportunities worth behaving for. The setting or mixing of groups is organised on a group-by-group basis to create healthy mixes of students. The curriculum is designed to cater for all interests and needs. Training for staff around positive discipline is ongoing. Time devoted to extracurricular activities is expanded.

- Join an academy chain because it feels it should. Instead, the school thinks about its contribution to the community it serves. It thinks through ways that the community can be alert to its qualities and the opportunities it can offer that community. The school makes itself indispensable to the community.

In Model Five, the driving force of the school is its teachers. Senior management understands that nothing can be achieved unless the teachers have ownership in the school and believe in what the school is trying to achieve. There is a genuine commitment to developing the skills of staff and keeping up to date with the latest thinking around teaching and learning.

The school is happy to learn with, and from, other local schools, without feeling the need to formalise that collaboration through chains, etc.

I hope that you don't think it folly to organise a school like this. This school has teaching and learning at its heart. That is an increasingly rare thing, which is sad. Teaching and learning are the very reason for the existence of schools. We are losing sight of this fact.

Where do you see your responsibility in all of this? Do you think you're just the NQT, and have to do what you're told? If that is your approach, then I take it that everything is fine at your school.

If everything is not fine at your school then I (we) need you to be involved, be active, in changing your school for the better. You can do this by being the best teacher you can in the classroom: always reflective about what you are doing, always looking outwards for support, always being vocal about the things you believe to be right.

You need to be brave. This new world of education works at the level of brutal and humiliating competition, thoughtless adherence to meaningless data, and narrowed student experience, based on preparing for high stakes stultifying exams. You are the new generation. Please help.

26

The regrettable language of education

And then ... they don't turn up to the exam. Are you accountable for that?

Teachers are encouraged (coerced, forced, required, begged) to provide data that indicates steady, incremental progress through levels. Is learning even remotely like this?

Are some topics more challenging than others?

Do some students have different levels of engagement for different topics?

Do students always feel equally up for school every day?

Do students always feel ready to be the level that the teacher has prescribed for them?

Why do we care about looking good? Is this a vicious circle?

England has some 20,000 secondary schools. Are they really all in competition with each other?

Should they all be aiming for the same thing?

Can education be reduced to a single formula that indicates success?

Here is a list of words and expressions that you need to treat with mistrust. Listen very carefully when you hear people using them. They are probably fobbing you off or hiding the truth or making excuses or going to humiliate you.

Accountable

Boys and girls, mums and dads: never ever allow yourself to be held accountable for the actions of other people's children. It is entirely right to take responsibility for the learning of the children in your classes. You should try to make the work as stimulating as possible. You should investigate ways of motivating and challenging your students. But you are not accountable for the actions of those students. You know the child you have backed all the way through school who no one else gave a hope for: the child you have bonded with, the one who sees you as the centre of their school experience. You have kept believing in them right through to Year 11. And then ... they don't turn up to the exam. Are you accountable for that?

Rigour

Shorthand for 'we must make school more unpalatable so that plenty of kids fail and accept, since they aren't bright, they must take that dead-end job'. Shorthand for 'we want an education that is based on the Industrial Revolution model; for the rich and able only'. Shorthand for 'we can't admit that in the rich environment of the information superhighway the children are just more alert, more informed, and this adds up to brighter; and this is the real reason that formal examinations results go up every year'. It is shorthand for a regressive curriculum that tests basic functionality. It is also shorthand for the head-in-the-sand attitude to the world which suggests that a British perspective is the only one to be trusted, and which deals a blow to any embracing of multicultural outlooks. Shorthand for 'mean-spirited'. You never hear a teacher say the word 'rigour' in the way politicians make use of it. This is because it doesn't make any meaningful, or purposeful, sense.

Data focus

Your school has a data monkey in it. He says things like, 'I have come to realise that data is the key to everything' and 'It will be fascinating to see how the children who get free school meals have done.'

All teachers know that data drives nothing at all that happens in the classroom. Most teachers pay lip service to data, dutifully filling in the electronic records of children's 'progress' and keeping a visible record of the marks in the back of their planners in case anyone senior wants to inspect what they are doing. Teachers know they can't trust the 'data' of the exam results, and all teachers are able to give a better account of the abilities of their students than any test or examination. I am also confident that all (most?) teachers understand that the 'sit down in isolation' examination that is still used to measure the ability of children serves no practical use whatsoever. The modern world does not require the capacity to remember information. Still, the data monkey wants to be fed with data. Teachers are encouraged (coerced, forced, required, begged) to provide data that indicates steady, incremental progress through levels. Is learning even remotely like this? Are some topics more challenging than others? Do some students have different levels of engagement for different topics? Do students always feel equally up for school every day? Do students always feel ready to be the level that the teacher has prescribed for them?

The truth is that data has very little to do with the students at all. It is about a school being able to justify its own systems and approaches by demonstrating that its students are making 'progress'.

Say to the data monkey in your school (normally a deputy head who is seeking promotion) that you would like to run an experiment. In Year 7 this year, let's have one group of children we never discuss levels with, that we never set learning objectives with, that we never spend time filling in learning logs with, that we never use any 'educational speak' with. We just teach the lessons, saying why they will be useful in the real lives of the students. Then at the end of the year let those children take the same tests as all the rest of the students who have been told they are a 4a, 6b etc. Observe your data monkey twitch at the thought that his whole existence may be entirely pointless.

Current climate

This is the catch-all excuse of those who seek to justify why situations in schools are unpleasant. It is a by-product of the credit crunch/austerity mentality. Unfortunately the use of this phrase has spread from senior managers to middle managers to the weary rank-and-file teacher. 'We'd like to do creative thinking and thoughtful lessons, but in the current climate ...'

People managing budgets, people managing the curriculum and, worryingly, people managing the fear of failure to deliver exam results for their students, all use this expression.

I have lost count of the times that a head of department has looked at me with a blank, uncomprehending stare when I ask them to encourage creative approaches to teaching and learning. 'In the current climate, Martin ...' Argh!

Learning journey

Journeys have endpoints. The expression is part of the whole reduction of education to the passing of exams. Interestingly, I think the expression is used with positive intentions. But it is euphemistic and weak. It reduces the responsibility of the speaker for educating children to the point when the children leave school rather than accepting the need to make education in school a starting point for lifelong learning. Its vagueness can also cover a multitude of sins; I suspect 'learning journey' often means being tracked by data.

Outstanding

While it may be becoming clear that I am less than satisfied with the way education policies are developing in this country, there also needs to be some soul-searching from those people in schools that I will call the 'Outstanding' chasers. You know who you are! You are the people who want to please Ofsted because in the 'current climate' you can't think of any other approach, or you don't have the strength of your convictions to try to run your school the way you know would work better. The word 'Outstanding' has been taken over by Ofsted and, ironically, fills teachers with dread, either because they are not deemed to be Outstanding or because they are, and they have to maintain this status. All teachers know there is no rhyme or reason to the offering of an Outstanding judgement to a school. It is the measurement of the unmeasurable by people who are not best fit (those would be the teachers actually in the school) to pass judgement on the competences of the school.

To even accept the word 'Outstanding' in a school is to accept the connotations that Ofsted loosely suggests. Schools that trumpet the fact that they are deemed Outstanding are merely saying that they have learned to do what they have been told, and that the education of their children has had to take a backseat in preference to making the school look good. Some schools that are deemed to be Outstanding don't trumpet the fact, but they tend to be the ones that get on with making a school rather than jumping through the Ofsted hoops. Why do we care about looking good? It is precisely because of the fear of the brutal, random and humiliating regime of inspection. Is this a vicious circle?

Reactive responses to Ofsted will not grow a school. 'Outstanding' chasers at all levels within schools present a genuine threat to education.

League tables

Let's think about league tables for a moment. The idea, I suppose, is borrowed from competitive sport. I suspect that it makes most people think of football. Should education be a competitive sport?

It strikes me that the very system of league tables builds in limitations. In English football there are ninety-two professional teams. Only four can win a league, only two can win a cup. The rest will be left frustrated by their lack of what they see as achievement (Tottenham?) and some will struggle constantly (Barnsley?).

In education there are four leagues (sponsored by Ofsted!). On the face of it, there can be many more winners.

Whatever budget or set of circumstances a school finds itself in, there is the opportunity to be in the top league. But we can't *all* be in the top league. However hard schools work, we won't put them all in the top league. The government would be attacked for 'coasting' (to use their own word), for lacking aspiration. A league system demands losers.

In a league system we are in competition. This breeds secrecy. We are not going to share our new initiatives or ways in which we have managed to achieve success. England has some 20,000 secondary schools. Are they really all in competition with each other? Should they all be aiming for the same thing? Can education be reduced to a single formula that indicates success?

To win a football league, you have to win more times and score more goals than every other team over the whole season. In schools the season lasts one hundred and ninety days, but your chance to prove yourself lasts two days. Sometimes you clearly have no chance to prove yourself because the verdict on the school is predetermined before the two days by your exam results and by political whim. Governments need schools to do badly so that they can 'fix' them.

'... even better if ...' etc. (yawn)

Where to start with this one? It would be 'even better if' teachers were not encouraged to use this empty, meaningless language. Making children think about their work in these formulaic terms reduces the capacity to think about their future potential. Children know what this is all about, and are quite prepared to play the game. After all, while they are filling in boxes on progress sheets saying 'even better if', they don't have to be doing anything. A bit of mindlessly being occupied will suffice now and again. Students would learn more about their progress by looking at their exercise books from the previous year and seeing for themselves whether they are making any advances.

Next up, we have a very wonderful word. However, you need to use it with caution. Be clear what you mean when you use it – and make sure the person you are speaking to has the same understanding. You'd be surprised.

Education

Whenever you are engaged in a conversation with a line manager about 'education', about 'teaching and learning', be careful. Most of the time, while you mean 'providing stimulating lessons that help children become resourceful adults', your line manager might mean 'getting children to pass examinations'. Politicians always mean 'measurable progress' or 'results', and senior managers in schools sometimes mean that too. Now, here is some space for you to insert a tenth word of your own!

27
Top ten teachers

Here's an activity for you to try.

Imagine that your school is to close down (these days, that isn't so very hard to do!). However, thankfully, you are going to reopen (hurrah!) – *but* you can only keep ten of your staff. Make a list of the names of the teachers you would keep. Next to each name, write down why you are keeping them and the qualities they bring to the school. What you are identifying is a mix of best practice. Here you have the very core of what makes your school the success that it can be at its very best. Take a long look at this list. It represents what you think is important. Given that you have identified these members of staff as the essentials at your school, next to their names write down a promotion that you could give them.

Cross out the names of the teachers and you will feel a little less guilty about the activity! What you have left is a checklist of what you value in a school. I wonder what your list says. Actually, I don't wonder what it says, because I have tried this activity over and over with educators. Most have a list of relationship-building qualities ('great with the kids', 'a real team player who gets the best out of her colleagues', 'really cares about his students'). Most have a sense of leadership and of staff being role models for both other staff and students. Just about everyone values what they call having a 'personality'; being inspirational and knowledgeable. I have found that student teachers and NQTs hardly ever stray outside these personal qualities. Generally, the interest in personal qualities totally outweighs concern for subject-based skills. Head teachers sometimes wish for a data monkey and a disciplinarian, but they generally also hanker after the same attributes as their teachers. Whoever we are, we seem to agree that what is important is the ability to forge meaningful relationships with students and staff alike. Does your list match up with my presumptions?

When reflecting on your own practice, you could perhaps circle the qualities you feel you already possess. Don't be modest: if you are 'good' with the kids then circle it. The things you haven't circled are the things you value but you feel you have yet to acquire. This then becomes a shopping list for your ongoing development.

Did you put yourself on the list? If you didn't, then you may want to reflect about why that is. Perhaps you were being modest again. Perhaps it didn't cross your mind that you were allowed to do that. Or perhaps you aren't in the top ten teachers at your school. If you don't think you are in that top ten, then it is time to look at the list of attributes that you *didn't* circle and set about actively pursuing them.

28

What influence can you exert in your school?

'We are not only responsible for doing our duty or for working for the good, we are also responsible for deciding what this good is ...' (Slavoj Žižek)[1]

How do you feel about the question above: what influence can you exert in your school? I have asked a lot of questions in this book, but this one is one of the toughest.

(Increasingly we see leadership models in which the senior management team in schools distance themselves from the rank and file. This can have a negative influence on how middle leaders and regular teachers feel about their potential to make a contribution to their schools. The NQT and the trainee have the added insecurity of being 'new', of being 'inexperienced'. It can be difficult to be vocal when you feel that your voice is not valued, or valuable.)

But you must believe in your influence in your school.

Most obviously, you have an influence in your own classroom. You set the agenda, the methods of study and the atmosphere. The mood in the room will normally be yours. Students tend to pick up on the moods of their teachers and respond accordingly.

You must have an influence in the corridor. Don't stop being a teacher the second the bell goes and your lesson is over. Students know the difference between teachers who

---

1 Slavoj Žižek, *Demanding the Impossible* (Cambridge; Polity Press, 2013).

care and those who are serving time. Chatting to kids in the corridor, sitting with them at lunch and putting on extra things for them to do, such as clubs, do not go unnoticed.

You must have an influence at departmental meetings. Be vocal, be positive. Contribute because you can. If you don't agree with what is happening, then say so.

You must have an influence the moment that you walk in the door. People will soon notice, and the credence of your voice will multiply. People will want to listen because you are a positive contributor. You have something to say and it is worth listening to because the children respect your attitude and the staff respect your commitment.

29

Agents of change

What about education? Should those new to the profession be changing it?

You are part of the new generation of teachers. Do you like what you see?

Are there ways that things could be done better?

Should I be suggesting such rebellion?

Where will student teachers and NQTs look for role models? It is the young that drive change to our language, developing the ways we speak and write. Contrary to popular belief, the young are not lazy in the ways they communicate. They are inventive with standard written grammar and vocabulary, and they are playful with the ways that they speak. One of the basic principles of language change has always been ease of articulation. Each generation changes the language they are presented with to make it easier to use.

What about education? Should those new to the profession be changing it? You are part of the new generation of teachers. Do you like what you see? Are there ways that things could be done better? Those trainee teachers I work with are always telling me how things could be improved!

Here's a thought. When student teachers enter the profession, one of the things I suggest is that they consider the ways things are and then think through how they are going to change things for the better. Should I be suggesting such rebellion? New teachers aren't always young, but they are fresh to the education system. They can perhaps perceive how things *could* be rather than how they *are*. Those within the system can very often become institutionalised, seeing only the ways things are. Perhaps student teachers and NQTs are best placed to observe and comment on practice in schools. In these days of corporate, formulaic school systems it is even more important that we listen to the new voices you represent. Speak up!

Student teachers and NQTs often tell me about their misgivings about what they are being expected to do. Departments and faculties have agendas that tend to serve the gods of passing examinations. This pressure is increasingly felt at primary school level as well as secondary. Competition to be the 'best' school in the area is measured largely by exam results. Fragmentation of supportive networks on the back of this competition further increases the drive to pass examinations. New teachers seem to be directed, more than ever, towards what they have to do. Often lessons are built around the learning of examination technique and content. If this persists, then we will be breeding a generation of unthinking school teachers for whom the matter of educating children will look like a simple process when it could – and must – be so much more.

Where will student teachers and NQTs look for role models? I work with student teachers and I know they are quick to spot the mechanistic approach to teaching. The constraints under which they are placed are still visible to the student teacher largely because they are offered the excuses about 'the current climate' and 'we'd like to but ...'. The appetite for change is there, but the weight of expectation to deliver short-term exam results is immense.

For me, the problem is that there seems to be a growing sense that you can either educate children or you can focus on exams. It is a brave teacher that puts this idea to one side and trusts her instinct. If you educate a child, then that child will be able to do the exam, without the exam being the focus of the study. I shall keep telling new teachers this is the case. That awareness is vital if we are to provide a fitting education for the times in which we live. Your students must amount to more than an examination result that advantages the school.

30
Sharing good practice

Here is an idea for you (at no charge). In the summer months (after the SATs in primary and when Year 11, Year 13, etc. have left secondary), invite all your teachers to contribute to a book that you will collectively produce. The idea is simple. Everyone writes about a success they have had in their classroom during the year. They write in whatever form they choose. Some might write a formal essay, quoting academic research. Some might give you a blow-by-blow account of what happened in a lesson or sequence of lessons, with an assertion about why it went well. You might even get some photographs of smiling children to put in the book. Others will tell you of a technique they are using throughout their lessons with different groups.

This activity will not be met with universal approval! Some won't want to commit to the activity because they can't see the point, some will say they don't have to do it, and some will (in all honesty) tell you that they don't have time to do it. Teachers who say they don't have time are actually telling you that they don't have any interest in developing their practice. Realistically, about a third of a typical school's teachers will feel that they would like to contribute to such an initiative. All you need then is a member of staff to take on the role of compiler/editor and you have yourself a brilliant little resource.

What is so good about this book?

1. Staff you have never heard say anything at all about curriculum might present their ideas for the first

time. This type of member of staff may feel liberated by the written page and the opportunity to draft and revise his ideas.

2. You hand the book out in the September staff meeting on the first day back at school, along with the timetables, planners and SEN notes for the coming year. The book says that the school cares about staff development. You can't make everyone contribute to the book, and you can't make everyone read it, but you can make it explicit that a teaching and learning opportunity was there. It is the sort of initiative that grows over time. More people will want to be in it the following year.

3. The good practice outlined in the book relates to students in your school at this moment. INSET trainers who visit school can tell you about stuff that might work in your school but this is actual examples that have actually worked; recently and right here.

4. Make it clear to parents that this book of good practice has been produced by the teachers. Announce its publication on the school website. Leave copies in the school foyer. Give copies to all the school governors. Stakeholders will soon get the idea that what they have is staff who want to grow their capability and who are pulling together to improve the standard of education that the school can offer.

5. You are involving staff in the act of writing and, by extension, reading about teaching. This requires reflection upon practice – measuring your own practice against those around you.

This is an idea that I have tried. It works, and it inspires confidence in the staff that they matter and that the school values the development of pedagogy.

31
After the NQT year

Where do you have the opportunity to develop your abilities?

Do you have access to authoritative role models?

Does your school keep up to date with theory?

Does it allow your department to have subscriptions to professional associations?

Do INSET and twilight sessions focus on the development of teaching and learning?

Do you genuinely have the energy on top of your mountainous workload?

Could a new National College for Education take on the challenge of fixing professional development at the centre of progression throughout teaching careers?

Could we create opportunities for teachers to do research in the classroom, to be seconded to teacher training institutions, to have time to write about and share good practice?

Could we pay more to teachers who successfully connect theory and practice?

Might teachers be given time and money to work on key areas of development, such as our approach to digital literacy?

At the end of your first year as a teacher you become qualified. You have joined the profession. All mentor support tends to be withdrawn, you are given a full timetable, and you are on your own. You are in the mainstream: expectations of your performance increase, and reliance on you to deliver the goods with teaching exam groups grows. You will benefit from the INSET days (about five a year), although much of this time may have been taken by senior management to pursue things other than developing the capabilities of their teachers (oh, the irony!). You could join the lunchtime teaching and learning group or a steering group thinking about the needs of the personal and social education (PSE) curriculum. But those books keep stacking up, and you don't know much about the next module of work with Year 5, and your group is going to organise a cake sale, so all that teaching and learning stuff will have to wait. Perhaps next year. Perhaps when you have a bit more time.

Time is the problem. There never is enough time, and then there is the fact that developing the understanding of staff around teaching and learning is not a short-term concern. It can always wait. But it is only put off because in some schools the development of staff is not a priority. In fact this is often, I am afraid, the case. Have a think about your situation. Where do you have the opportunity to develop your abilities? Do you have access to authoritative role models? Does your school keep up to date with theory? Does it allow your department to have subscriptions to professional associations? Do INSET and twilight sessions focus on the development of teaching and learning?

Training teachers is vitally important throughout the whole of their careers. The needs of the pupils move on, the curriculum should be moving on and new research uncovers more about how we should be learning. And yet it is true to say that, once your NQT year is over, you don't have to engage with any notion of taking your practice forward. You are trained and that is that. Unfortunately, performance management and performance related pay are fixed on how you are doing now, not on your potential to develop. I suppose it would be true to say that the profession relies upon your professionalism to keep you up to date and thoughtful. But do you genuinely have the energy, on top of your mountainous workload? Possibly not.

The development of teacher competences has to be at the centre of education. Training is extremely important during this time of great change. We cannot afford to keep seeing release time to go on a course as a 'treat' for the teacher. We can't keep relying on teachers to organise TeachMeet events. Actually, at the moment we *can* rely on this sort of activity. It exists because the teaching profession will always find ways to encourage the sharing of good practice. But it is a symptom of the fact that the current state of affairs discourages such collaboration. Lunchtime is a time to eat and rest, rather than to cram in training opportunities. We can't keep working in isolation, school set against school, in a competition to be the best.

We need a coordinated approach to ongoing training throughout your teaching career. Could a new National College for Education take on the challenge of fixing professional development at the centre of progression throughout teaching careers? Could we create opportunities for teachers to do research in the classroom, to be seconded to teacher training institutions, to have time to write about and share good practice? Could we pay more to teachers who successfully connect theory and practice? Might teachers be given time and money to work on key areas of development, such as our approach to digital literacy?

32
In conclusion

What do children need from a
twenty-first-century education?

Can we galvanise the teaching of
English and ICT to make sure that students
are literate in the truly modern sense of
that concept?

Can we develop the ways in which students
approach the use of the internet?

Can we help them to be healthily sceptical
and shrewd in their judgement of what they
are looking at?

Can we support students in making
creative uses of the internet, past simply
accessing information?

Can we support their understanding that
the internet can be a learning resource?

Can we look at the curriculum again?

Can we develop a curriculum that
supports a useful perspective of the world
around our children?

Which areas of scientific advance
should be considered?

There is a growing worry about obesity in the UK. Apart from PE, where else on the timetable can we counter this problem?

Let's take a look at the current state of affairs in our education system. What follows is a highly personal view – but then I take it very personally. Having been a teacher for over twenty-four years, I have seen this landscape evolve and have seen its contours take shape. It is important to be clear about the wider world of education to which you have committed.

Whether you agree or not is not the issue for me. What is important is that you have an opinion about what follows.

Things in schools have changed in many ways in recent years. Short-term-gain political interference has increased remarkably. The role of Secretary of State for Education has become a key position in government rather than a safe outpost. Education is a battleground of politics.

The teaching of basic skills is at the forefront of this battle. Current policy, and therefore curriculum design, is about the knowing of facts. Creative thinking and self-reliance are proving difficult skills to value in these pressurised days of competition. And how remarkably short-sighted this is. Businesses are crying out for imaginative thinkers, but instead are being offered students who are good at learning. This leaves you in your classroom with a challenge. You must teach the required facts but do so in a way that is engaging to the students and useful to them in their future. You have to help students pass exams that require rote remembering of facts. However, more importantly, your students need the capacity to join in with an adult world that has little time for such an outdated skill. While your students must 'know' facts, you can use this background to foreground the skills they will need in their adult lives.

The government (and, I suspect, the next government as well) wants all schools to be autonomous, saying that each school should have the chance to govern itself. In reality this leads to competition instead of collaboration. Good work – your work – is being repeated and duplicated everywhere, rather than shared. Pressurised leadership in schools tends not to think for itself, but looks to what it should be doing. The range of state schooling narrows. Every school has recently invested in signage and mottos: 'Aspire and Achieve', 'Aspire to Achieve' and the like repeated over and over again; all indicative of this narrowing of provision in the state sector. You must see past this competitive environment to help secure a department and a local group of schools that collaborates, sharing good practice and always being open to the ways other practitioners operate.

Inspection of schools today is brutal and humiliating. Ofsted hovers over schools like the plague. Its judgement is punitive, its impact draining. It seems to teachers that Ofsted sits in judgement, but offers virtually nothing in terms of lessons learned (excuse the pun!). The goalposts keep being changed: Ofsted judges individual lessons – then it doesn't. Ofsted wants to see individual lesson plans – then it doesn't. Ofsted needs a percentage of Outstanding lessons before it can award Outstanding status – then it doesn't! Ofsted dictates what makes an Outstanding lesson – then it doesn't! Do you have the strength of character not to crumble under this intense scrutiny? Accept advice about what an inspector has seen, but do not seek to beat yourself up about criticism. The inspector saw twenty minutes of your lesson, and her judgement and comments do not in any way reflect on your capacity as a teacher.

The examination system has lost all sense of trust. Over the past few years the reputation of examinations has fallen into disrepute. The media cries out that exams are getting easier, the exam boards change the marks needed for grades after the exams are taken – and sometimes in the middle of a course – and teachers are accused of cheating.

Government and exam boards pull teachers in different directions and the three groups never talk productively to each other. Please make sure that you do not focus entirely on exams in producing your schemes of work and lesson plans. Exams are no more than gauges of what and how well something is learned (and most of the time they are inadequate at doing that!).

Inequality across schools is part of the tiered system that now exists. We see schools dropping out of local authority control to become academies so that they can have a larger share of funding. We see schools with brand new building next to schools that aren't really fit for human habitation. We see the national curriculum requirements being made of state schools – unless they are academies. Academies don't have to follow the national curriculum. Work that one out, if you can.

There is a movement of teacher training from university-centred provision to schools being given the leading role. With very limited financial support and no training for staff, schools are being asked to train the next generation of teachers. Teacher training is better done 'on the job', apparently. Just like if you were going to be a fireman: best just to turn up at a fire (oh, hang on ...). This amounts to a de-professionalisation of teaching. Whenever you meet a new colleague, make it your job to enhance their development, regardless of the route by which they made it into teaching.

And yet in lots of ways things are in need of further change.

The basic curriculum hasn't changed since the 1890s. Education is not really keeping pace with the changes needed in the workforce. In the drive to improve basic standards of literacy and numeracy and the insistence on a narrow exam-focused curriculum, the creativity and resourcefulness that leadership in industry requires is proving elusive. Top companies are becoming wary of students who have achieved all A*s at school because it is largely a sign that those students are successful at doing what they are told. Make sure that you are offering relevant experience in your classroom. Ask yourself what the value of your lesson is to the student. When they leave the classroom they should be richer in some way for the experience they have just had.

Technology has also left education behind. We are at a generational point when young people are much more skilled than the adult generation in making use of technology. Much of the adult generation is wary of social media, frowns upon the innovative ways that young people adapt language to suit their needs, and lacks the ability to use the opportunities that computers offer (past replacing the library and the typewriter). Your lesson must reflect the ways in which your students communicate in the real world outside the school gates.

Young people's perceptions of what a career might be have changed. There are fears that new teachers do not stay in the profession very long. However, gone are the days when young people left school with the idea that the job they would do would be a job that they expected to do for life. We are having more career changes in our working lives. The teaching profession needs to take this into account.

Teachers are characterised in the news as 'demoralised'. But fear not: we are a hardy bunch. Teachers working in classrooms with children are among the most dedicated and optimistic people on the planet. *They understand that they offer hope.* The problems and pressures outlined above are all peripheral to the shared experiences of the classroom. You can still make your classroom a happy and vibrant place to be, despite the pressures you face.

As you set out on your career, entering the teaching profession is newly complex. As mentioned before, the government has decided to dismantle the university-led model in favour of all kinds of choices and all kinds of providers. The experiences of your new colleagues may well be very different from your own.

Training of new teachers needs to be taken seriously if we are to provide a community of teachers capable of equipping our young people with the skills and outlooks they require to prosper in their adult lives. We need an effective system.

Unfortunately, *there is no system at the moment.* The government has created a fragmented and unbalanced free-for-all that is unregulated and unsafe. Student teachers are having vastly different experiences. Some are receiving thoughtful and useful tuition, while others are being used in schools as cheap labour. Some people are working as teachers without any qualifications or training at all. This last set of circumstances has to stop immediately. There should be a well-understood and clearly defined set of expectations that all new teachers need to demonstrate a commitment to and for which they have a competence. This is not the case at the moment. Pointing to the eight Teachers' Standards is not a good enough response, as not all teachers have had to prove anything against these 'standards'.

The teaching profession should have a central core. You should be joining a community of professionals, all of whom should have the same collective goal: enhancing the education of all children everywhere. Lip service can be paid to this aim now, but it cannot flourish in the brutal atmosphere of competing schools. Teachers must make sure they stand together in the pursuit of the best education possible for our children and for their futures.

As you join the profession, you need the widest possible insight into the potential that different schools can bring to improving and developing educational practices. You need to be able to visit schools of different phases (primary, secondary, college, etc.), serving differing social backgrounds and communities, and with different areas of expertise. You also need to be able to share your experiences with experienced colleagues and with other new teachers.

You need forums in which you can discuss what you have seen and to share your thinking about ways forward. Newly qualified teachers should be entitled to work with qualified and experienced teacher educators whose job it is to support their learning. I don't mean a teacher who has taken on this role alongside a full teaching commitment. I mean a trained teacher educator with the time and competence to train the next generation of teachers.

You need to be able to see the wider professional community (if indeed it still exists past TeachMeet events) you are joining. In school-based training the emphasis is often on training for a specific school or group of schools. This is a narrow introduction to the potential that a career in teaching might have, however. There is a good deal of angst at the moment regarding the fact that too high a percentage of entrants to the profession only stay for a short time. While there are a number of other reasons for this, I am sure that teachers offered this narrow perspective of teaching do not see the variety of opportunity that teaching across the UK can offer. Make sure that you take every opportunity to work with other schools. Speak to feeder primaries/high schools, go to TeachMeet events, go to subject events run by the LEA or exam boards. The professional associations of subjects should be the focal points of curriculum development. You need access to theoretical research to inform the pedagogical approaches you adopt. You need the opportunity to share successful resources and lesson planning ideas. You need subject support groups. You need to keep up to date with developments to the syllabuses on offer. You need opportunities to contribute to the wider community of subject-based sharing hubs.

What do our children need from a twenty-first-century education? Communication skills appropriate to the digital highway seem to me to be the number one aspect of learning relevant to the environment in which our children are growing up. Can we galvanise the teaching of English and ICT to make sure that students are literate in the truly modern sense of that concept? Can we develop the ways in which students approach the use of the internet? Can we help them to be healthily sceptical and shrewd in their judgement of what they are looking at? Can we support students in making creative uses of the internet, past the accessing of information? Can we support their understanding that the internet can be a learning resource? Most children use the internet as a source of entertainment.

I believe that the most pressing issue facing teaching is how teachers should teach. As I watch lesson after lesson in UK schools, I am struck by the increasingly narrow range of teaching methods being employed. The four-part lesson plan is creating formulaic approaches that are repeated lesson after lesson. The interpretation of the buzzword 'pace' means that lessons are packed with, frankly, pointless and often unexplored activities. This has the side effect that children never really get to reflect on what they are doing and hardly ever get to look back at what they have achieved. The tokenistic filling-in of evidence that reflection has been done is almost always a waste of time. There is also a tyranny of writing: endless writing down of stuff that is not needed for any reason other than to prove that something has been done. Please be thoughtful about the systems you are offered. Consider carefully the value of the forms, data sets and routines of your school. Be vocal when things work and when they do not.

You need more licence to do what you know your students will benefit from and you need the opportunity to be thoughtful about how to teach. To support this we need to put core professional development and links to the most recent research at the centre of what we do. You need to be well informed about current research into how the brain works. You need to have access to research findings. You should be able to conduct research projects of your own. Research initiatives and projects should be tied in to your career progression. Those teachers who take steps to inform themselves about developments in educational thinking should be rewarded. There should be more collaboration between schools. The isolating impact of 'competition' is a major barrier to this. Imagine how much excellent work is being done in staffrooms and departments around the country – and no one outside the school ever gets to hear or benefit from it. If we are to persist with inspection bodies, such as Ofsted, then part of their remit should be to make sure that they share the good practice they observe. This could be done every month through all sorts of media.

Can we look at the curriculum again? Can we develop a curriculum that supports a useful perspective of the world around our children? Given that a sense of history helps a child locate herself within her culture, what will be the important (relevant) times and cultures to deal with? The growing importance of China on the world stage might suggest that we should examine that culture. The constant tensions of the Middle East might suggest that a unit on revolution and on ideology could be necessary. Geography may need to concentrate on environmental issues, but which? Science develops so rapidly. Which areas of scientific advance should be considered? There is a growing worry about obesity in the UK. Apart from PE, where else on the timetable can we counter this problem? Think about the contribution that you and your subject can make to the whole education of a child.

Our education system at the moment is fixated on the learning of basic skills which, frankly, are largely innate; and in the case of some (for example, grammar), under threat of becoming irrelevant as technology enhances our capacities. We need to pursue a framework that supports educators to develop children: for economic reasons, for cultural identity, for social engagement and for personal development. I suspect the old model of distinct subject lessons is now getting in the way, as is the idea of testing students individually. We need project-style work that ranges across the subject disciplines and that encourages collaborative, interdependent working.

Our world is changing around us faster than ever before. While this presents challenges, it also means that the world is an exciting prospect for the generation of children in schools right now. Can the teaching establishment respond?

Here are the main challenges I can see in the future for education in the UK – and for you in your classroom.

What it means to be literate is changing. Digital citizenry is the major growing means of communication. Over the past few years the issue of getting everyone online has been the challenge. However, the focus for technology is no longer to do with the need for universal access, but the need for digital literacy. Your ability to handle online applications is going to either include or exclude you. Schools need to operate in this new environment, and they need to support their students to help them join in.

The short-term goals of elected governments make long-term educational stability incompatible with political involvement. We need *a National College for Education* run by teachers and academics with the remit to support the work of schools. Such a body should look to support the work of all schools by sharing good practice. The National College should also actively seek to get schools to work collaboratively to develop pedagogy.

Ofsted inspections need to be overhauled to become formative, rather than summative, in the judgements they make on schools. The judgements should not characterise the whole school as they do at the moment. Reports should detail only what is good enough or not good enough about the practice of a school. In those areas where negative judgements are being made, Ofsted should offer useful advice based on good practice seen in other schools. Failing this, Ofsted should be scrapped and the new National College should regulate schools. Schools need to stop chasing the Outstanding label. This suggests that a school is good at doing what it has been told to do: nothing more. Teachers need to be encouraged to see Ofsted's comments as mere snapshots of an individual visit rather than career-threatening indictments. It is important that you see Ofsted in this light.

Regardless of the resources available to a school (and being mindful of the ways in which students are more receptive to learning when the environment is right), the real driving force for learning in the room is the teacher. Teacher education is vitally important if we are to re-professionalise this career. All teachers must be qualified and have demonstrated a minimum set of competences. University-led courses, with work experience in schools, remains the best way to develop this quality assurance. A single route to becoming a teacher is the way to make sure there is equity of provision. It will also help to make sure that the supply of teachers reaches the level of demand.

Teachers who engage in ongoing core professional development should be rewarded for this commitment to their own practice, and the collective initiative of improving teaching and learning. Research projects and collaborative initiatives with other schools or authorities should be remunerated with time and pay implications. Core professional development should be linked to pay rises.

To my mind, the top priority for education is to move it away from the remit of politicians. Politicians should not be setting the agenda. They are not the best-placed group of individuals to think through the needs of our children in the twenty-first century. They aren't even having the conversation that is needed. When politicians talk about education they seem to be talking about short-term examination successes, not the education of children as a preparation for adult life. The discussion of what children should learn is mixed up with the idea of 'British-ness'. Look at the ridiculous mention of 'British values' in the Teachers' Standards. This inevitably leads to a narrowing of focus when, in these global times, we should be facing outwards. The actual art of teaching receives very little attention; indeed, the current government doesn't seem to think there *is* much art to teaching. Concentrating on why, how and what (in that order) to teach are essential as we move forward.

The world is radically different to how it was when our education system was devised. The world has changed, and now we need to change to meet its needs and demands. And it is going to be up to you, my new colleague, to start sorting it out.

... what are you going to do about it?

Good luck. Enjoy your teaching!

'My mate says you're a great teacher.'

Walking into a pub, I am hailed by a couple of young men standing outside having a drink.

'Mr Illingworth, you taught my mate.'

'Oh right. Good.'

'He says you're great. Best teacher he ever had.'

'That's nice.'

'You made him count the railings!'

And it's true. I did send a lad out to count the railings because he was getting on my – and everyone else's – nerves. Funny how children don't always remember – or value – the pearls of wisdom you thought you were imparting.

Index

H

habits of mind 31
hope 3, 99, 159
Hooley, N. ix
humour 36, 60, 96

I

imagination 69–72
internet 20, 47, 48, 49, 50, 74, 79, 114, 155, 162

K

knowledge 9, 15, 19, 20, 27, 34, 48, 56, 57, 65, 66, 79, 95, 99, 100, 105, 106, 115, 141

L

lesson planning 2, 3, 10, 11, 13, 21, 59, 88, 91, 107, 157, 158, 162
listening 32

M

market values ix, x
memory/long-term memory 21, 50, 61, 79, 84
mistakes 30, 37, 99, 101, 118, 124
motivation 88, 90, 115

N

No-Brainer Academy 111–112
newly qualified teacher (NQT) 13, 125, 127, 131, 141, 143, 145, 146, 151–153

O

observation 13
Ofsted 2, 3, 13, 24, 66, 111, 128, 129, 130, 131, 137, 138, 157, 163, 164, 165

P

PGCE 12, 120
passion 9, 10, 12, 30, 100, 101
pedagogy 12, 118, 119, 150, 164
persisting 31–32
personal philosophy 63–68
policy xii, 67, 129, 156
pressure 13, 36, 42, 65, 89, 130, 146, 159
professional development (*see also* core professional development) 3, 151, 153
progress 10, 19, 27, 52, 69, 70, 73, 105 111, 130, 133, 135, 136, 139, 140, 151, 153, 162
purpose xii, 2, 3, 8, 10, 11, 18, 22, 26, 43, 48, 52, 67, 75, 89, 115, 117, 130, 135

Q

qualifications (*see also* PGCE) 122, 160
questioning 23, 34, 55–58

978-1-78135-055-3

Bringing together some of the most innovative practitioners working in education today

www.independentthinkingpress.com